T0301708

Purpose-Driven Pricing

Pricing is frequently used as a key strategic lever for management to increase profitability. However, price can also be used as a lever for societal good. This book demonstrates how effective use of price can have positive societal impacts, such as helping to reduce carbon emissions, accelerating the adoption of eco-friendly products, and improving people's health outcomes and quality of life.

This book, written by two leading thinkers on pricing strategy and practice, makes the important link between the ideals of purpose in organizations and the crucial tools of how to implement change using one of the fundamental levers at the disposal of the organization. It introduces the concept of leveraging the power of pricing for both profit and societal good and then clearly explains how it can be done. Price can be used to manage demand, incentivize consumer behavior, and influence change. The impact can be effective and quick, and it is not far-fetched to say that pro-social pricing can be utilized to preserve the environment, educate citizens, promote arts, alleviate poverty, and improve health. The book outlines how corporations, governments, civil society organizations, and collaborators can use pricing power to manage the adoption of products and services across B2B and B2C. Pricing strategies include innovating, unbundling, unpackaging, collaborating, implementing new monetization models, and applying learnings from behavioral pricing.

Executives of corporate and business strategy and those dealing with brand portfolios, sustainability, social and health equity will find profound insights in this book. It will also be valuable in executive training and for graduate students.

Saloni Firasta-Vastani is a seasoned consultant and a professor at Goizueta Business School at Emory University, and teaches pricing strategy and monetization curriculum to graduate, executive and undergraduate programs. She is a frequent speaker and commentator at industry conferences and on the radio, TV, and print media channels, such as NPR, CNN, Fox, ABC, and NBC.

Jagdish N. Sheth, Charles H. Kellstadt Professor of Marketing at Goizueta Business School at Emory University, has over 350 publications. A global marketing luminary, he is the recipient of PD Converse, Padma Bhushan, Parlin, and Wilkie Awards.

"In today's market, integrating Diversity Equity and Inclusion (DEI) strategies into business models is not just a moral imperative but a competitive advantage. *Purpose-Driven Pricing* brilliantly encapsulates this ethos of aligning pricing with core values, ensuring accessibility while sustaining business growth. This book is a must-read for leaders striving to create purpose-driven economic models without sacrificing excellence or profitability."

Shan Cooper, *CEO Journey Forward Strategies;*
Previous Chief Transformation Officer, West
Rock Company; Previous VP & General Manager
Lockheed Martin

"The idea of variable pricing in the cultural sector is becoming increasingly relevant as venues attempt to establish more sustainable operating models and foster greater equity. This is an important tool that cultural organizations will need to have in their toolkit as they plan for the future."

Henry Kim, *Michael C. Carlos Museum Director*
and Associate Vice Provost, Emory University;
Director and CEO Aga Khan Museum Toronto (previous)

"As a technologist, I see many doors opening for new strategic options in pricing practice. Purpose-driven pricing offers new thought and a rich roadmap for strategically leveraging these capabilities and neglected opportunities in service of commerce and society – for profit and social good."

Benn Konsynski, *Professor and technologist,*
Goizueta Business School, Emory University

"The authors of *Purpose-Driven Pricing* skillfully blend theoretical concepts with practical applications, making it an invaluable resource for businesses striving to innovate purposefully in competitive markets. Its unique approach to pricing as a key element of innovation is a game-changer, providing readers with the tools to create value for customers, organizations, and society. A must-read for anyone involved in business strategy and innovation."

Craig Dubitsky, *Founder, Hello Products; Former Chief*
Innovation Strategist, Colgate-Palmolive

Purpose-Driven Pricing

Leveraging the Power of Pricing for Profit and Societal Good

Saloni Firasta-Vastani and Jagdish N. Sheth

Routledge
Taylor & Francis Group

LONDON AND NEW YORK

Designed cover image: Getty Images/RollingCat

First published 2025
by Routledge
4 Park Square, Milton Park, Abingdon, Oxon OX14 4RN

and by Routledge
605 Third Avenue, New York, NY 10158

Routledge is an imprint of the Taylor & Francis Group, an informa business

British Library Cataloguing-in-Publication Data
A catalogue record for this book is available from the British Library

Library of Congress Cataloging-in-Publication Data
Names: Firasta-Vastani, Saloni, author. | Sheth, Jagdish N., author.
Title: Purpose-driven pricing : leveraging the power of pricing for profit and societal good / Saloni Firasta-Vastani and Jagdish N. Sheth.
Description: Abingdon, Oxon ; New York, NY : Routledge, 2024. |
Includes bibliographical references and index.
Identifiers: LCCN 2023056986 (print) | LCCN 2023056987 (ebook) |
ISBN 9781032658940 (hardback) | ISBN 9781032634814 (paperback) |
ISBN 9781032659008 (ebook)
Subjects: LCSH: Pricing--Social aspects.
Classification: LCC HF5416.5 .F57 2024 (print) | LCC HF5416.5 (ebook) |
DDC 658.8/16--dc23/eng/20240112
LC record available at https://lccn.loc.gov/2023056986
LC ebook record available at https://lccn.loc.gov/2023056987

ISBN: 978-1-032-65894-0 (hbk)
ISBN: 978-1-032-63481-4 (pbk)
ISBN: 978-1-032-65900-8 (ebk)

DOI: 10.4324/9781032659008

Typeset in Sabon
by SPi Technologies India Pvt Ltd (Straive)

From Dr. Saloni Firasta-Vastani

To Minaz and our children
Zibran and Sanay, who light up our life
To my mother and father for letting me dream

From Prof. Jagdish N. Sheth

To Rajendra (Raj) Sisodia who is the Cofounder of
Conscious Capitalism and strongly believes that business can
positively serve the society through purpose and passion.

Contents

Preface

In its simplest terms, price is the amount of money that's exchanged when goods or services pass from the seller to the buyer. The buyer views it as the amount they must part with or sacrifice to get what they need or want. The seller views it as a means for increasing profit and market share. However, price is not only a key lever for financial performance for a company but also a key factor in the customer's decision to purchase the product or service. Both parties agree to the price but are ultimately looking out for their own interests. Simple, right? Not necessarily. In this book, we will look at price in a different way. We will ask the question: *What if we could leverage price to change the world for the better?*

This book explores how pricing can be leveraged to improve quality of life, improve the environment, and even reduce traffic. Using versatile pricing strategies such as bundling, unbundling, and implementing new monetization models, we show how price can provide a win–win solution for businesses, the planet, people, customers, collaborators, and overall society.

For centuries, businesses have existed to fulfill customers' needs and increase their quality of life, from railway companies that transported goods to department stores that sold everything from livestock feed to garments to modern food delivery services that bring meals to the front door. At their core, businesses strive to please and delight their customers in exchange for a price. From these efforts stem competition, with businesses constantly striving to provide higher value than other companies, building products that customers enjoy more and ultimately are willing to pay a higher price for. As a result of this narrow definition of price, maximizing customers' willingness to pay has become the mantra of many businesses, regardless of how much it costs to society and the planet to deliver that product or service.

However, in the last few decades, customers are becoming more concerned with what goes on behind the scenes: *How did the firm produce the product? Do they have ethical business practices? What is the state of their corporate citizenship?* Corporations have come forth to fulfill this social expectation of the customers, and the idea of Corporate Social Responsibility (CSR) has gained popularity. Additionally, governments are becoming more aggressive in the debate over corporate roles and are bringing forth regulations for how companies conduct themselves. Firms are accelerating their efforts to find ways to do the right things for not only their customers, but also for humanity and the planet while remaining profitable. A few things in the external context are also driving companies to make these changes sooner rather than later:

- In November 2022, both the EU Parliament and the European Council granted official approval for the EU Corporate Sustainability Reporting Directive (CSRD). Scheduled to become a legal force in 2023, it will be put into practice during the fiscal year 2024 for larger companies. This directive mandates companies to *meticulously document and disclose their ESG* (economic, social, governance) endeavors, employing metrics specified by the European Financial Reporting Advisory Group (EFRAG). The vision behind the CSRD lies in enhancing corporate transparency, harmonizing sustainability norms, and motivating enterprises to enhance their commitment and investments in sustainable practices. This collective effort aims to expedite the shift towards a more sustainable economy.
- In 2015, United Nations Member States unanimously embraced the 17 Sustainable Development Goals (SDGs), including a comprehensive spectrum of objectives to be achieved by the target year 2030. The SDGs acknowledge that *eradicating poverty* must be seamlessly entwined with tactics *fostering economic advancement* while also attending to diverse social requisites like education, healthcare, equality, and job opportunities.

How did our book come about with all of this as the backdrop? The idea of pricing for societal goods first entered our radar in the summer of 2021. The idea came about while working on a consulting project for a company, GreenPrint, that was working on launching a new type of credit card. GreenPrint had a simple value proposition: they would plant trees to offset the carbon footprint, and customers would pay them to do so. For example, the card calculates the carbon deficit created by the customer's gas purchase at the pump, and the company automatically offsets it for a small fee. We were tasked with determining the card's annual fee, considering the customer's willingness to pay and market share penetration. We conducted comprehensive primary and secondary research to develop our recommendations. Through surveys and conjoint analyses, we concluded that there were two options—both of which would result in similar financial outcomes for the firm.

- Option 1: Price the card at an annual fee of $96, with an expected market share of 10%.
- Option 2: Price the card at $48, with an expected market share of 25%.

After much discussion, thought and deliberation, we determined that the second option, to price the card at $48 or $4 per month with the higher market share expectation, is superior. Why? With a neutral impact on the financial bottom line, this option offered a solution with more trees being planted, which is better for the planet. This simple yet additional variable of including the society and planet in the decision-making was missing in the initial business case. The lesson learned was this: If societal and planet concerns are incorporated into the business case, managers may make a different decision in light of this new perspective. This project marked the concept's inception, which is at the heart of our book *Purpose-Driven Pricing*. Dr. Sheth, whose research in sustainability has been recognized worldwide, and is a legend in the marketing discipline for his work related to relationship marketing and conscious capitalism, was a natural and excellent choice for guidance to shape the idea into the book we have today.

The book is divided into three sections:

Part I: The forces behind purpose-driven pricing
  In Part I, we discuss our knowledge so far, such as understanding real costs to society, behavioral pricing, managing innovation, and tailoring pricing strategies to fit the lifecycle of products. This discourse centers on wielding our current knowledge to forge pro-society strategies *without* forsaking business goals. We discuss the seven-point plan to implement change.
Part II: Bringing stakeholders along
  Part II delves into the collaborative orchestration of government entities, consumers, people, and stakeholders within the value chain. This journey discusses pathways for collective engagement, leveraging existing resources, and championing a unified transformation trajectory. Through real examples and best practices, we share key learnings.
Part III: Case studies
  The final part unveils seven pricing tactics fortified by real-world cases that can help managers adopt them in their own organizations.

We support cultivating a broad perspective, encouraging thought-fulness, wisdom, and compassion as we navigate tradeoffs between society, individuals, employees, and investors. Companies are society's economic engines, and we hope managers take both short-term and a long-term views when making these pricing decisions so that the tradeoffs benefit society, people, employees, and investors. The lessons contained within this book are timely and can be directly applied to help companies accelerate their social and environmental performance while minimizing financial tradeoffs and, in many cases, improving financial performance.

Acknowledgments

We express profound gratitude to Rebecca Marsh at Routledge for her swift recognition of this book's potential. Her unwavering support, guidance, and seamless facilitation have been invaluable in this process. Our thanks extend to Dean Bargh for his prompt reviews and constructive insights. Special recognition goes to Chuck Davenport and Alpa Sutaria for their significant contributions to Chapter 7, enriching content that resonates even within the context of B2B enterprises.

We're thankful to Emory University Jeff Rosenzweig, whose mentorship and support proved instrumental in completing the research. Professor Sheth thanks his research assistants, Canon Harty and his administrative assistant, Angel Harris, for their support. Dr. Firasta-Vastani thanks her student, Zach Nusbaum, Jacob Housen, Himanshu, and several others, for their work and feedback on the book.

Personal gratitude resonates from Dr. Firasta-Vastani for her husband Minaz, her children- Sanay and Zibran, her parents and mentors. Sanay, your constant encouragement and balanced and logical feedback steered this work. Zibran, your ideas, and insights on your generations' perspectives were thought-provoking, pushed me to think about the issues deeply. Minaz, your patience, love, and unwavering belief in me have been the bedrock of this endeavor. My mother, Zarina, your fearless spirit, and my father. Pyarali your wisdom and service to the community inspire me daily. I am deeply grateful to Prof. Sheth for the thirty years of guidance and mentorship, from encouraging me to get a doctoral degree and publishing this book.

We hope you find this book useful in providing the concepts and ideas you can implement to avoid making the necessary tradeoffs to keep businesses thriving. Providing customers with good value, not at the cost of people and society, will create goodwill, admiration, and a thriving business. We hope to usher in a better world for the next generation with this multilateral perspective. We are only on this planet for a short time – let's leave it better than we found it.

Contributors

 **Chuck Davenport** is an Expert Partner at Bain & Company, based in the Atlanta office. He has over 20 years of consulting experience in pricing and related commercial excellence disciplines. He is also an experienced operating executive with functional experience in pricing, procurement, finance, and sustainability. Chuck holds an MBA from Goizueta Business School at Emory University and a Bachelor of Electrical Engineering from Georgia Tech.

 **Alpa Sutaria** is the Senior Vice President of Corporate Strategy & Sustainability at WestRock, where she works with the company's leadership to chart the course for transformation and growth support of WestRock's purpose: "Innovate Boldly, Package Sustainably." Alpa previously worked with Coca-Cola across various strategy, finance, marketing, and revenue management roles for 20 years, and has experience in management consulting and paper manufacturing. Alpa holds a BS in Operations and Industrial engineering from Cornel and a MBA from Goizueta Business School at Emory University.

Part I

The forces behind purpose-driven pricing

1 Pricing for societal impact
Why does it matter?

A cynic knows the price of everything and the value of nothing.
Oscar Wilde, *Lady Windermere's Fan*

For much of the 20th century, business strategy traditionally revolved around aligning various functional areas to realize long-term profitability for the firm and its investors as the primary goal and, furthermore, the firm's only responsibility. This was enshrined in the now-famous 1970 essay by Milton Friedman in the *New York Times*: "The Social Responsibility of Business is to Increase Its Profits." Taking aim at the nascent corporate responsibility movement, he asserted that a company's responsibility should remain solely to its shareholders, with no obligation to the wider society or the environment. However, in recent years this viewpoint has been widely and consistently challenged. A broad acceptance has emerged since this article was published that a corporation is indeed responsible for people and the planet as well as profit. In fact, these ideas have become so mainstream that we are witnessing a backlash or "woke capitalism" from those who believe that companies' sole responsibility is profit.

In this new landscape, corporations and their managers have a new range of challenges and ethical dilemmas: tough decisions must be made and tradeoffs navigated. In recent years, the notion has resurfaced that social responsibility and the long-term viability of the business are entirely incompatible goals; many managers still adhere to "old-school" patterns of thought despite changing attitudes across society. It is, therefore, a matter of urgency for managers to understand the context within which they are working. They need the right forward-thinking training so they can incorporate both purpose and profit into their core decision-making framework. Only then can they ensure the long-term viability of both their business and wider society – without forsaking one for the other.

In this chapter, we will examine at the importance of profit aligned with purpose and then explore the idea from a pricing perspective. In the following chapters, we will examine best practices,

DOI: 10.4324/9781032659008-2

frameworks, and case studies which will illuminate on the kind of training a manager needs to operate and make decisions within a forward-thinking pricing framework.

Aligning purpose and profit

First, we should acknowledge that not all corporations are on the same page. The recent "anti-woke" rhetoric, alluded to earlier, is doubling down on the traditional Friedmanesque philosophy and remaining unapologetic about a profit-only stance – even in the face of evidence of environmental or societal damage. Such a mindset sees societal considerations as a dangerous distraction from a business's core purpose.

The context of such skeptical attitudes is one in which companies across the globe remain all too willing to inflict damage on society and the environment. In the last few years, we've seen some examples include Archer Daniels Midland, which engages in developing biofuels but is facing legal challenges amounting to hundreds of millions of dollars on account of pollution issues. As reported by *Newsweek*, its environmental footprint is considerable, and its reputation ranking is below average. In addition, its executives were in violation of various laws and involved in a price-fixing scandal. Nestlé has faced criticism for its aggressive marketing of infant formula in developing countries, leading to reduced breastfeeding rates in areas with unsafe drinking water – with disastrous consequences for infant health. Monsanto (acquired by Bayer) has been criticized for its production of genetically modified organisms (GMOs) and the controversial herbicide Roundup, which has been linked to environmental and health concerns. The investment company BlackRock recently came under fire for recruiting a Saudi businessperson to its board of directors. BlackRock has been a vocal supporter of the environment and uses it regularly as an investment evaluation criterion, so an association with Saudi Arabia, a country often criticized for its human rights violations, was not well received.

And so, writing this in 2023, despite huge progress in adjusting the 20th-century corporate paradigm to align with a sustainable future, the "business case for sustainability" debate rages on. Clearly, though, in the face of incontrovertible evidence about the harm that irresponsible businesses cause, the question is not *why* to try to do good for the people and the planet – but *how*: how to manage the tradeoff between responsibility and profit. There needs to be a robust decision-making framework for aligning the two objectives, both in the short and the long term. We believe pricing plays a pivotal and yet little-understood role. This book will explain how pricing can be the lever to align profit and purpose.

The relationship between profit and pricing

In 2014, Deloitte Consulting LLP launched its "Exceptional Company" research project with the aim of establishing the factors behind long-term exceptional performance in companies. The study examined all publicly traded companies based in the United States from 1966 to 2010. In all, 347 companies were investigated and categorized as either exceptional, mediocre, or poor performers. Through quantitative analyses and in-depth case studies, the behaviors of exceptional performers were compared with those of companies of average lifespan, performance level, and performance volatility.

Their conclusion? "[A] near term focus on profitability rather than revenue growth offers a surer path to enduring exceptional performance." In other words, companies with a higher profit margin have greater long-term sustainability – you can survive and thrive if you have sufficient profits to reinvest in the company. Your company can only make a difference so long as it continues to exist!

The findings revealed that exceptional performance was primarily dependent on superior differentiation and higher revenue, often achieved through higher prices. No other factor was consistently significant. In fact, exceptional companies were characterized by a willingness to make significant changes to their businesses – transformations even – if it meant they would maintain their differentiation and revenue advantages.

Three rules emerged from the research:

1. *Better before cheaper*: Instead of competing on price, focus on delivering superior value to customers.
2. *Revenue before cost*: Drive profitability by increasing price and volume rather than relying solely on cost reduction.
3. *There are no other rules*: Adapt and align with rules 1 and 2, employing any necessary strategies to sustain differentiation and revenue leadership.

These simple rules offer a glimpse into the mindset and strategies of exceptional companies striving for long-term success. To make it in the long term while continuing to serve your customers, provide employment, and provide returns to your investors, a focus on profit is critical. However, as we later evaluate, profit and purpose are not mutually exclusive or compete with each other.

Pricing has a critical role to play in every firm's profitability. A 1992 McKinsey study looked at over 2000 companies across many industries. It weighed the impact on profit of a number of factors, among which was: how much would profits be impacted by a 1% improvement in price, costs, or volume (i.e., increase price or volume by 1% or decrease variable or fixed costs by 1%)? On average, a 1% improvement in unit volume led to a 3.3% increase in operating profit, assuming no decrease in price. A 1% improvement in price, assuming no loss of volume, saw a 11.1% increase in operating profits (see Figure 1.1). The unequivocal conclusion is that improvements in price typically have a huge impact on a firm's profitability.[1] In fact, companies can increase their profitability by anywhere from 20% to 50% by systematically implementing of the right pricing strategy.[2] In recognition of the importance of price as a driver for revenue and profit, many Fortune 500 companies have dedicated pricing groups.[3]

As well as having the biggest impact on profit, price is also a significant influence on customers' purchasing decisions, with several research studies confirming that price is *the* primary consideration.[4] Not just a key variable at the customer decision point, price can even be (and often is) used to steer customer behavior: higher prices deter consumers; lower prices incentivize people to buy more. Companies can dynamically adjust prices to manage demand:

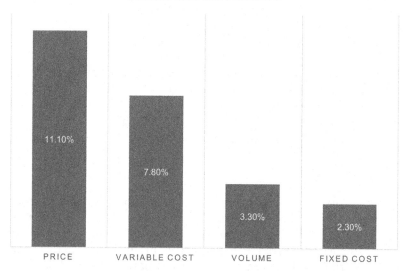

% COMPARISON OF PROFIT LEVERS WITH 1% PRICE IMPROVEMENT

Figure 1.1 The influence of a 1% improvement in price on profit levers.

Source: Michael V. Marn and Robert L. Rosiello, September–October 1992. https://hbr.org/1992/09/managing-price-gaining-profit

Note: Chart values based on average economies of 2463 companies in Compustat aggregate.

charging more when anticipating high demand or stimulating demand by lowering prices. Airlines have used dynamic pricing techniques in this way for decades: in the 1990s, they increased their profitability by over 8% by using pricing as a lever to manage inventory. Hotels followed suit and, in turn, have boosted their profitability by over 5% with closely managed prices.

Corporate purpose

"Corporate purpose" as an idea is a relatively new addition to the business vocabulary. Some terms often associated with corporate purpose are Corporate Social Responsibility (CSR), ESG (Economic, Social, and Governance), sustainability, DEI (Diversity, Equity, and Inclusion), the Triple Bottom Line, and Stakeholder Capitalism. Now commonplace in the business lexicon, these would nonetheless have been quite unfamiliar only a few decades ago and are largely a result of a rise in consumers' environmental awareness which began in the 1970s. ESG reporting standards, for example, which were developed and published in the 1980s, were spurred by a series of environmental crises and the governmental and citizen action that followed.

In the last couple of decades companies have been making public commitments with the aim of enacting the idea of corporate purpose. For example, a publicly declared Corporate Social Responsibility goal might be to achieve carbon-neutrality; more recently, companies have aligned with social causes, such as gender equality and inclusivity. Campaigns promoting these goals (for both company internally as well as those aimed at customers or shareholders) are usually freely accessible to the public. Below are some examples of companies who are making a commitment to society and planet.

As a mark of its commitment to responsible water practices and water stewardship, Coca-Cola aims to replenish the water it uses in its products and processes. The company also focuses on community development, supporting various educational and environmental programs worldwide. In 2010, over 300 million individuals in Africa were grappling with insufficient water and sanitation facilities. As a response, Coca-Cola launched the Replenish Africa Initiative (RAIN) to provide access to safe water to two million people in Africa by 2015. Over time, the goal expanded to improve both clean water and sanitation access for six million people with a proposed additional $35 million in investment. This endeavor aligns with United Nations Sustainable Development Goal 6, which is to "Ensure access to water and sanitation for all."

Walmart promotes sustainable sourcing practices, which include buying sustainable food and favoring ethical supply chains. It aims for a positive social and environmental impact by reducing its greenhouse gas emissions and increasing its use of renewable energy. With a goal of being 100% powered by renewable energy, the company has invested heavily in solar and wind energy projects for its stores and distribution centers. Walmart also endeavors to reduce waste: it has plans to reduce plastic waste and is pledging to make its private-brand packaging 100% recyclable, reusable, or compostable by 2025. On the supply chain side, it is encouraging manufacturers to move to environmentally and socially sustainable practices; specifically, it provides incentives for suppliers that comply with Environmental, Social, and Governmental (ESG) standards. In 2023, after several months of inflation-related price increases, the company rejected any further increases from its manufacturers to keep its stores affordable.

Unilever has a reputation as a corporate "good citizen." Having become known for its "Sustainable Living Plan," it has set ambitious goals to improve health and wellbeing and reduce its environmental impact. It commits to sustainable sourcing and waste reduction and also undertakes social initiatives. Through its various community programs, it works with its suppliers to ensure standards are upheld throughout the value chain. Unilever has attained a reputation for its sustainability initiatives while keeping its prices reasonable – using innovative channel marketing, packaging, and sourcing to manage costs. Alan Jope, Unilever CEO, declared in 2021 that doing business sustainably and ethically has not been more costly; in fact, the benefits have outweighed the costs.

Lego, the iconic toy brick company, is a pioneer in sustainable investments. In September 2020, it pledged over $400 million to achieve complete sustainability in its packaging by 2025. This fund will also be used to support other projects, such as the "Learning Through Play" initiative, which educates children about environmental issues, as well as strategies aimed at reducing its global environmental footprint. Furthermore, Lego has committed to transitioning to fully sustainable production practices by 2030, ensuring that its toys are manufactured with minimal impact on the environment.

Purpose-driven companies are far more common in today's 21st-century corporate culture. Their philosophy directs the firms' objectives and plays an important role in employee morale, talent attraction, brand loyalty, and collaborator value.

The relationship between profit and purpose

Corporate purpose, when effectively integrated into a company's strategy and operations, can contribute to long-term profitability.

At first, incorporating social purpose may result in higher costs and reduced profits. However, in the long run a clear and authentic corporate purpose can yield several benefits that positively impact long-term financial performance. Here are some ways in which corporate purpose can contribute to sustained profitability:

1. A strong corporate purpose that aligns with the values and aspirations of customers can foster *customer loyalty and trust*. Customers are likelier to choose and remain loyal to companies that demonstrate a genuine commitment to a larger purpose beyond profit. This can lead to increased customer retention, repeat business, positive word-of-mouth, and overall financial growth.
2. When employees feel a sense of purpose and alignment with the company's mission, they tend to be more engaged, motivated, and committed. *Engaged employees* are often more productive, innovative, and customer-focused, which can drive efficiency, quality, and long-term profitability.
3. A well-defined corporate purpose can help *attract and retain top talent*. An increasing number of employees seek meaning and purpose in their work, not just a paycheck. Companies with a clear purpose are more likely to attract talented, passionate individuals who are aligned with their values, resulting in a more skilled and dedicated workforce that positively impacts the bottom line.
4. A purpose-driven company is often more flexible and able to adapt to changing market conditions. A strong sense of purpose can fuel *innovation*, inspire creative problem-solving, and encourage experimentation. This enables companies to anticipate and respond to evolving customer needs, stay ahead of competitors, and seize new business opportunities.
5. A company with a genuine commitment to corporate purpose tends to build a *positive reputation and strong relationships with stakeholders*, which include customers, employees, investors, communities, and regulators. A favorable reputation can enhance a company's brand value, attract investment, and foster positive partnerships, all of which contribute to long-term profitability.

Several organizations are trying to quantify the impact of these changes and building case studies to document the impact. Incorporating the financial impact in the return on investment calculations will enhance the viability of these projects.

The triple bottom line

Many companies choose to share their progress on their commitments. A triple-bottom-line *report*, also known as a sustainability report, is a comprehensive   document   that   measures   an   organization's performance in three key areas: economic, social, and environmental. The concept of the Triple Bottom Line (TBL) recognizes that a company's success should not be evaluated solely on financial metrics but should also include its impact on people (social) and the planet (environment). Such a report, typically including data, metrics, goals, initiatives, and targets in each of the three areas, gives a company's stakeholders – including investors, customers, employees, regulators, and the wider community – a comprehensive overview of its sustainability performance and shows how it is managing its economic, social, and environmental responsibilities. It can help stakeholders make informed decisions and hold the company accountable for its impacts.

- The *economic* dimension assesses the organization's financial performance, including aspects such as revenue, profitability, and economic value added. It examines how the company creates economic value for shareholders, employees, and other stakeholders.
- The *social* dimension evaluates the organization's impact on society, employees, customers, and communities. It examines aspects such as labor practices, employee wellbeing, diversity and inclusion, community engagement, human rights, and philanthropic initiatives.
- The *environmental* dimension focuses on the organization's environmental impact, including resource consumption, emissions, waste generation, and efforts toward sustainability and conservation. It assesses the company's environmental management practices, initiatives to reduce its ecological footprint, and contributions to mitigating climate change.

Across the line, many companies from various industries now publish triple-bottom-line or sustainability reports to communicate their economic, social, and environmental performance. Whether it be Unilever's "Sustainable Living Plan," Coca-Cola's "Environmental and Social Initiatives" booklet, Nestlé's "Creating Shared Value" report, or Novartis's "Corporate Responsibility Report," these companies' efforts at maintaining transparency highlight their commitment to sustainable and ethical practices. Investors, customers, employees, regulators, and the wider community all benefit from these voluntarily published reports.

However, companies that have effectively incorporated societal considerations into their business strategies often find that the long-term benefits outweigh the initial expense despite the unknown returns on early investments. In fact, several studies (see below) have confirmed that purpose-driven companies come out ahead in the long run. Books such as *Firms of Endearment* and *Green Giants* contain case studies of such firms, i.e. Chipotle or

Patagonia.[5] However, in the short term, very often managers at the frontline do not always fully understand the tradeoffs and inevitably struggle with the necessary decision-making. They may not be aware of the reasoning behind these decisions or fail to see how the incentives align with the overall objectives. Even in companies where managers are fully aware of the firm's goals, the managers are not always trained on how to balance these seemingly conflicting priorities – how to align purpose and profit.

The financial case for purpose

Our research has found that the integration of corporate purpose and financial performance varies according to industry, company size, specific circumstances, and motivations. Societal benefits are often brought into the calculations when discussing product differentiation or when recruiting talent. Despite the variation, there are some common drivers behind the profit of purpose-driven enterprises, which may include the following:

- A study by IBM[6] found that, on average, 70% of purpose-driven shoppers pay a premium of at least 35% for sustainable purchases, such as recycled or eco-friendly goods. Similarly, the NYU Stern Center for Sustainable Business found that consumers, on average, pay 25–29% more for environmentally friendly goods and services.[7] Ethical and sustainable practices, as well as commitment to the community, are critical qualifiers driving consumer loyalty and purchasing decisions.
- The NYU Stern Center for Sustainable Business's research[8] also found that 50% of the growth of consumer-packaged goods between 2013 and 2018 came from sustainability-marketed products. Research from GreenPrint[9] found that nearly 80% of consumers are more likely to purchase a product labeled environmentally friendly, with 77% of those surveyed saying they are concerned about the environmental impact of the products they buy.
- Having a purpose can drive up investment valuations. Brands with a higher sense of purpose have experienced a brand valuation increase of 175% over the past 12 years, compared to the median growth rate of 86%.[10] These numbers can be incorporated into the overall business case.
- Many large investment firms and banks are now investing only in companies that provide benefit from social and environmental perspectives. Private equity and market investors are paying more attention to the overall impact of the firm and value and support companies that are driving positive change on the frontline.

Since this topic first came to general notice in 1953,[11] *"purpose"* has gained traction in both academic literature and praxis. While it is viewed as a source of competitive advantage,[12] the benefits to brand equity, employee engagement, and long-run success are still somewhat unclear and more needs to be done on quantifying the impact. Smaller firms need to understand the implications if they are to make financially astute decisions[13] because they typically lack the cash flow of the bigger corporations – which is needed for longer-term decision-making.

A 2011 *Harvard* article[14] discusses the tangible benefits of Corporate Social Responsibility (CSR), such as competitive advantage, reputation, authenticity, and employee engagement. However, in spite of numerous claims along these lines, we've found it hard to find a quantifiable measure of return on investment. Most results are survey-driven and measure the stated preference of customers alongside a company's actual experience. Such evidence as is currently available does indeed validate a robust connection between long-term profitability and CSR, but there is a scarcity of research on effectively reconciling CSR with *short-term* profitability. Furthermore, knowledge about formulating a purpose-driven business case is still in its early stages.

Aligning price, profit, and purpose

When we first started discussing with managers that pricing could be the key to integrating purpose, it seemed like a weak link. However, once we shared a few anecdotes about the relationship between price and purpose, a deep underlying connection between the two concepts started to emerge with our audience. The idea of pricing for profit has been normalized in the business world for decades. However, we are entering a new era in which three bottom lines, not one, measure a corporation's success, and we need a forward-thinking way of incorporating this concept into our firms' DNA and their management techniques. Figure 1.2 shows the various areas in which pricing can improve societal outcomes in addition to profits (1) and revenue growth (2) which we discussed earlier in the chapter. Below are a few stories showing how pricing can evolve and be leveraged for profit and for the betterment of society. So far, we have discussed the relationship between profit and price and also between profit and purpose. In this section, we introduce the idea of price in a broader context other than just how it influences profit.

Pricing for demand management

As well as serving as a key lever for profit, pricing can also be used as a lever to manage demand. As we mentioned above, it

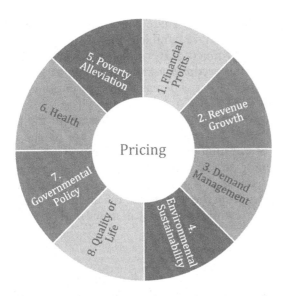

Figure 1.2 Pricing for profit and beyond.

exerts a major influence on customer behavior – which is often used expressly to manage, with higher prices deterring consumers and lower prices incentivizing people to buy more. We used the example of airlines, who have been using these dynamic pricing techniques to manage their demand and boost profits. Many cities are using dynamically priced fast lanes to manage traffic and to keep cars moving in that lane: the price to use a fast lane varies according to the time of day, e.g., going up at rush hour. Parking meters in Santa Monica, near Los Angeles, are designed to dynamically price parking bays in order to reduce demand during peak times and combat congestion. The higher prices encourage delivery vehicles and any other drivers with time-flexibility to park during less busy periods. The area benefits from reduced traffic and better air quality – thanks to the demand-management power of pricing.

Pricing for a sustainable environment

Based on research by NYU Stern Center for Sustainability using 2021 transaction data from retail stores. It shows that the market share of sustainable grocery store items in various categories is growing at over 50%. The Stern Center for Sustainability report shows that sustainable products have captured a notable 17.3% market share, showing a positive growth of +0.3 percentage points compared to 2020. Despite the context of a high inflationary environment, their market share continues to increase. Moreover, sustainable products have exhibited impressive growth, outpacing non-sustainable products. Over the last five years, sustainable products achieved a commendable Compound Annual Growth Rate (CAGR) of 9.43%, whereas their conventional counterparts managed only 4.98%.

As we saw above, consumers who care about the environment will speak with their wallets. And there are plenty of them! In 2021, 49% of consumers said that in the previous year, they had paid a *premium* (an average of 59%) for sustainable or socially responsible products.[15] These ethical products are often launched at a higher price from the outset, and the additional profit potential has enabled firms to further invest in other initiatives.

Pricing for poverty alleviation

In his book *The Fortune at the Bottom of the Pyramid*,[16] C.K. Prahalad described how multinational corporations' (MNCs') involvement in the poorest nations can not only benefit the MNCs by providing profits but also improve the lives of people who live there. The traditional Western capitalist mindset is to serve those who can pay, while the poor must be protected and subsidized by the government and non-governmental organizations (NGOs). Prahalad proposes a different approach in which the poor, the company, *and* the environment all benefit.

He presents a new approach to *alleviating poverty* by partnering with the poor to find innovative solutions and improve the price–value performance for this segment. An example is the success of Ala in Brazil, where a higher-quality product at an affordable price point brought profits for Unilever and improved clothes washing performance for the poor. Unilever designed its new product with key attributes such as extra power to whiten clothes but, crucially, adjusted the packaging and the size to appeal to and be affordable to this segment. Showing how businesses can tap into the market potential of low-income people in emerging nations and simultaneously improve the lives of those people, Prahalad's book argues that the poor, who constitute what he labels the "bottom of the pyramid" (BOP), represent a large and untapped market opportunity for businesses if they can offer affordable, good-quality products and services. He also discusses the role of civil society and government in this endeavor, which is something we will turn to in the latter part of this book – pricing strategies can even have an enormous impact on helping nonprofits accomplish their purpose.

Many MNCs are leveraging the idea outlined by Prahalad. They are becoming increasingly innovative with their products and improving price–value performance. For example, in 2007, Home Depot faced a difficult decision about whether to offer paints that were cheaper yet harmful to the environment. It was one that demanded careful consideration, as withdrawing the product had both revenue and profit implications. They eventually decided against it: their viewpoint was that irrespective of consumer demand, the company would not be acting responsibly by offering such products. In order to manage their assortment, they instead lowered the margin on the next-most expensive paint so as to offer consumers a lower-priced option. The increase in sales volume, and hence revenue, of that product compensated for the loss in margin and the costs of removing the harmful paints.

Companies such as Georgia Pacific, Coca-Cola, Walmart, Chipotle, Toyota (Prius), and Nissan (Leaf) are also successfully bridging the affordability gap to enable the penetration for eco-friendly products. Later in the book, we will be discussing some of the solutions these firms and others have developed to offer goods and services available at affordable prices to improve market penetration.

Pricing for healthy living

In a 2013 study, researchers from the U.K. and from Tufts University, MA, created a tool called the U.S. IMPACT Food Policy Model. It included projections of U.S. demographics and cardiovascular-related death rates to 2030. They combined that data with current and projected fruit and vegetable prices. The model simulated the effects on eating behaviors of different prices. They found that a 30% reduction in the price of fruit and vegetables can save 200,000 lives over 15 years. It is a clear indication that making healthier foods more affordable will save people's lives as well as provide massive healthcare cost savings. So, will we as a society be facing more cardiovascular disease at the end of this inflation run? The answer is likely yes and the higher associated costs will likely be more than the subsidies we could provide to lower the price of healthy products. A strategically developed pricing strategy that adds value to consumers at all income levels could be of more help.[17] Discounts or food stamps to low-income segments of the population could be one strategy, but that will likely not be sufficient or effective for broader society. Simply lowering prices across the board for everyone may not solve the issue – fruit and vegetables need to be made more accessible and convenient and, more importantly, in the first instance, people have to be persuaded that it's a good idea to buy them.

In 2022, fast-food prices increased by 7% on average, while grocery store prices grew by about 12%. With supermarket food purchases outpacing fast food, people will likely resort to eating fast food for more meals. Fast-food restaurants, such as McDonald's, reported no loss in customers during this period; in fact, they reported an increase in transactions while prices increased by 7%. The impact of this trend on issues such as obesity, diabetes, and cardiovascular health is severe. A worsening of public health outcomes is one of the longer-term consequences of continuing inflation. This is not to blame McDonald's or other fast-food restaurants but rather to illustrate the importance of management of grocery prices to incentivize healthier diets.

Pricing for governmental policy

Tax policies can be effective in gaining some quick wins in addressing public health issues. A classic case is the tobacco industry, where in the U.S. a 10% increase in cigarette prices resulted in a reduction in use of 2–5%. In the younger population the effect was two to three times greater.[18] A student-led study conducted in the U.K. on alcohol prices demonstrated that an increase in price per unit of alcohol resulted in not only decreased consumption but also a reduction in violence.[19] Higher taxes on sugary drinks could potentially result in similar benefits. And to return to the issue of fast food, perhaps fries at a fast-food outlet should be taxed at a higher level to discourage consumption?

Pricing for improving quality of life

Novel business models and policies could also improve equality of access to public and private enterprises such as parks, museums, and the arts. This can foster the longer-term survival and flourishing of public goods. Public parks are important locations in which people can convene in natural surroundings. Museums, too, can be important free-to-access public spaces, as well as fulfilling their role in educating and promoting art and culture. However, in many parts of the world public spaces such as these are poorly maintained and end up as venues for illegal activity. The development of sustainable financial options and new monetization models could be the means of improving the long-term quality of life and thriving arts and culture in societies around the world. We discuss more about this in later chapters.

The seven-step plan

The purpose of this chapter was to introduce pricing's role as a mediator between purpose and profit. In the following chapters, we present the "how to": describing best practices, research, and cases to help you accomplish this goal. The material can be used in a step-by-step fashion to help you progress steadily (see Figure 1.3). However, you can also skip chapters and go to the one that is most applicable to your own business situation.

a) Step 1: Get *internal* alignment of external goals and understand "true" costs (Chapter 2).
b) Step 2: Evaluate the *lifecycle* stage of the product/innovation and develop a pricing strategy for that stage (Chapter 3).
c) Step 3: Understand *behavioral pricing* and adapt monetization and pricing models to align with customer psychology (Chapter 4).
d) Step 4: Be aware of government policy in your industry and look for governmental/NGO support and subsidies (Chapter 5).

Figure 1.3 The seven steps to purpose-driven pricing.

e) Step 5: Engage with *collaborators* to support their transformation along the value chain (Chapter 6).

f) Step 6: Manage context, *social norms*, and people's price expectations (Chapter 7).

g) Step 7: *Apply* pricing strategies and tactics to revise pricing in practice (Part III).

The rest of the book is dedicated to elaborating each of these steps in turn, along with relevant case studies and research. There are a number of case studies in this book, showing how companies have successfully addressed this challenge using strategies that might involve: innovating; unbundling; unpackaging; collaborating; changing monetization models; using new pricing strategies; applying learning from behavioral pricing; and, of course, reducing costs without reducing value.

Key takeaways

Managers today face a dilemma. Purpose and profit may seem irreconcilable goals since a firm's business strategy is often not aligned with its corporate purpose or social responsibility.

- Price is a key lever for companies, and a small change can significantly impact the bottom line. For most companies, however, price is simply an economic tool to influence profit. Few firms effectively use the power of price to create change. Not only can price be used to improve profits and market share, but it can also manage demand, incentivize consumer behavior, and influence change to purposeful ends.
- When this powerful lever is used for societal good, the effect can be inspirational and the impact swift. Pricing can be a tool to preserve the environment, improve quality of life, promote healthy living, alleviate poverty, and improve healthcare access.
- The crux of the question we address in this book is this: *How can we use the power of price to trigger purpose-driven behaviors, ultimately bringing about better outcomes for people, for the planet, and for the firm itself?*
- In this chapter, we introduce the seven steps for transforming a company to purpose-driven pricing with a short- and long-term viewpoint

Notes

1 Michael V. Marn and Robert L. Rosiello, "Managing Price, Gaining Profit." *Harvard Business Review Magazine*, September–October 1992. https://hbr.org/1992/09/managing-price-gaining-profit

2 K. Mitchell, "The Current State of Pricing Practice in U.S. Firms." Opening Speech, Professional Pricing Society Annual Spring Conference, Chicago, 2011.

3 Andreas Hinterhuber and Stephan Liozu, "Is It Time to Rethink Your Pricing Strategy?" *MIT Sloan Management Review* 53(4) (June 19, 2012). https://sloanreview.mit.edu/article/is-it-time-to-rethink-your-pricing-strategy

4 Sanjeev Varki and Mark Colgate, "The Role of Price Perceptions in an Integrated Model of Behavioral Intentions." *Journal of Service Research* (February 1, 2001). https://www.semanticscholar.org/paper/The-Role-of-Price-Perceptions-in-an-Integrated-of-Varki-Colgate/b63894237bc078d3e121abf1ea0a72b302fd8db2

Chiranjeev Kohli and Rajneesh Suri, "The Price Is Right? Guidelines for Pricing to Enhance Profitability." *Business Horizons*, 54(6) (November–December 2011). https://doi.org/10.1016/j.bushor.2011.08.001

5 Raj Sisodia, Jag Sheth, and David B. Wolfe, *Firms of Endearment: How World-Class Companies Profit from Passion and Purpose* (1st edn; Wharton School Publishing/Pearson Education, 2007).

Freya E. Williams, *Green Giants: How Smart Companies Turn Sustainability into Billion-Dollar Businesses* (AMACOM, 2015).

6 IBM, "Purpose and Provenance Drive Bigger Profits for Consumer Goods in 2020." The IBM Institute for Business Value (IBV), January 10, 2020. https://newsroom.ibm.com/2020-01-10-IBM-Study-Purpose-and-Provenance-Drive-Bigger-Profits-for-Consumer-Goods-In-2020

7 Randi Kronthal-Sacco and Tensie Whelan, "Sustainable Market Share Index: 2021 Report." NYU Stern Center for Sustainable Business, April 2022. https://www.stern.nyu.edu/sites/default/files/assets/documents/FINAL%202021%20CSB%20Practice%20Forum%20website_0.pdf

8 Ibid.

9 GreenPrint Holdings Inc., *Business of Sustainability Index* (March 2021). https://greenprint.eco/wp-content/uploads/2021/03/GreenPrint-Business-of-Sustainability-Index_3.2021.pdf

10 Kantar Consulting, *Inspiring Purpose-Led Growth* (2020). https://kantar.no/globalassets/ekspertiseomrader/merkevarebygging/purpose-2020/p2020-frokostseminar-250418.pdf

11 Howard R. Bowen, *Social Responsibilities of the Businessman* (Harper & Row, 1953).

12 Archie B. Carroll, "A History of Corporate Social Responsibility: Concepts and Practices." In A. Crane, D. Matten, A. McWilliams, J. Moon, and D.S. Siegel (eds.), *The Oxford Handbook of Corporate Social Responsibility* (Oxford University Press, 2008): 19–46.

13 Elizabeth C. Kurucz, Barry A. Colbert, and D. Wheeler, "The Business Case for Corporate Social Responsibility." In A. Crane, D. Matten, A. McWilliams, J. Moon, and D.S. Siegel (eds.), *The Oxford Handbook of Corporate Social Responsibility* (Oxford University Press, 2008): 83–112.

14 Matteo Tonello, "The Business Case for Corporate Social Responsibility." Harvard Law School Forum on Corporate Governance, June 26, 2011. https://corpgov.law.harvard.edu/2011/06/26/the-business-case-for-corporate-social-responsibility

15 Jane Cheung, Catherine Fillare, Cristene Gonzalez-Wertz, Christopher Nowak, Gillian Orrell, and Steven Peterson, "Balancing Sustainability and Profitability." IBM Institute for Business Value, 2022. https://www.ibm.com/thought-leadership/institute-business-value/en-us/report/2022-sustainability-consumer-research

16 C.K. Prahalad, *The Fortune at the Bottom of the Pyramid: Eradicating Poverty through Profits* (1st edn; Wharton School Publishing, 2004).

17 Jonathan Pearson-Stuttard, Piotr Bandosz, Colin D. Rehm, Jose Penalvo, Laurie Whitsel, Tom Gaziano, Zach Conrad et al., "Reducing US Cardio-vascular Disease Burden and Disparities through National and Targeted Dietary Policies: A Modelling Study." *PLOS Medicine* (June 6, 2017). https://doi.org/10.1371/journal.pmed.1002311

18 Centers for Disease Control and Prevention, "Economic Trends in Tobacco." July 26, 2022. https://www.cdc.gov/tobacco/data_statistics/fact_sheets/economics/econ_facts/index.htm

19 Institute of Alcohol Studies, "Rising Alcohol Prices behind Drop in Violence." April 23, 2014. https://www.ias.org.uk/news/rising-alcohol-prices-behind-drop-in-violence

2 Seeking internal alignment and true costs

A penny saved is a penny earned.

Benjamin Franklin

When setting a price for a new product or resetting a price for an existing one, a manager's primary focus is on the key metrics, such as potential market share and profit margin. However, quantifying a pricing decision's impact on society – let alone considering its ESG (Environmental, Social, and Governance) reporting impact – is something that few managers are currently doing. Even in those companies in which "Purpose" objectives reside as part of its overall Corporate Social Responsibility goals, decisions are typically made in silos across various functional areas. So, you may often find that one department is trying to do the right thing for the environment and society while the rest focus solely on profit or growth. For example, in the early 2000s, BP launched a high-profile rebranding campaign to showcase its green initiatives, with the tagline "Beyond Petroleum." Critics quickly pointed out that the company was still heavily invested in fossil fuels, and the rebranding was clearly more about improving its public image than a genuine commitment to renewable energy. When functional and operational decisions are made, their impact on society is rarely considered across the firm. When evaluating the success of a product launch, for example, the benchmark is routinely a set of profit or growth objectives. In many cases, socially responsible firms – or socially responsible managers within those firms – are typically perceived as having insufficient grounding in financial reality; social responsibility is often viewed as an extra cost burden. In this context, it's hardly surprising that many leaders lack an in-depth understanding of how to incorporate the social impact of pricing into decision-making frameworks to manage short- and long-term financial objectives.

DOI: 10.4324/9781032659008-3

Internal misalignment issues

Traditionally, "Purpose" has been used as a means of enhancing a business's reputation. Such efforts manifest themselves in charitable contributions, for example, or public relations programs. These initiatives are often disconnected from other areas of the company. Although such practices can improve external legitimacy, they may not necessarily yield the most favorable outcomes for society or, indeed, the business itself in the long run.

Taking an example from our own business consulting experience. A student entrepreneur once approached us to share a new business idea: a jacket with a special pouch! At that time, there were no products like it, and a pouch on a hoodie jacket was a key differentiator. Additionally, the jacket was made from sustainably sourced materials and produced by well-paid laborers. It was a promising concept that aligned with the growing demand for eco-friendly clothing.

However, on looking more closely, we stumbled on a critical issue: the packaging. The entrepreneur had gone for an extravagant presentation: a large, ornate box adorned with bows and decorative elements. Numerous extra items, like koozies and postcards, were to be found inside, most of which customers would likely discard as waste. Clearly, the entrepreneur was thrilled about the product and believed all this elaborate packaging justified the high price point of $250 for a jacket. The idea was that the packaging would convey the notion of luxury and exclusivity, attracting customers who were willing to pay a premium.

From the point of view of business advisors and potential customers, there was an inescapable contradiction between the product's sustainable ethos and the excessive waste caused by the packaging, which detracted from the very image the entrepreneur was seeking to establish – that of an environmentally responsible and ethically conscious product.

The entrepreneur was intelligent and had the potential to make this venture successful – the problem stemmed from a misalignment within the company. It appeared that the group responsible for developing the packaging had not been adequately informed about the firm's overarching mission to promote sustainability and responsible consumption. For a business and its products to thrive, cohesion and consistency are required across all its departments. A product's success depends not only on its features and quality but also on how well every aspect aligns with the brand's values and customer expectations.

In our advice to this entrepreneur, we stressed the importance of creating a unified vision for their company. It is crucial to ensure that all teams, from design to marketing, are on the same page regarding the firm's commitment to sustainability; by aligning the packaging with the brand's values, the entrepreneur could create a cohesive image that resonates with environmentally conscious consumers. As a result of the consultation, the firm revised its packaging to align product and purpose better.

There is a valuable business lesson here. This anecdote shows how small missteps and miscommunications can lead to significant consequences for a company's image and reputation. Businesses that want to succeed in today's market must pay careful attention to internal alignment so that every aspect of their operations reflects their commitment to social and environmental responsibility. Having learned these lessons, the entrepreneur's business idea was poised to become a sustainable fashion success story.

Many scholars have emphasized the importance of "Purpose" as an inherent part of the company's DNA rather than an isolated peripheral activity.[1] However, in our experience, most firms' operations are still not integrated enough to deliver results across all departments, and this sparks conflict and tension between functional areas. Perhaps the finance department is too profit-focused while marketing are too preoccupied with market share?

This was the case for Ralph Lauren when its profits were eroded in the early 2010s. The marketing and finance departments had ended up at odds with each other at a time when the company was pursuing a policy of aggressive expansion, relying heavily on the sale of discounted items at department stores and outlets. By 2017, the realization dawned that these lower prices were hurting brand value – and hence profitability – and the discounting was brought to an end. Ralph Lauren's shares recovered by 10% – although it suffered a sharp decline in sales in the first quarter of 2017 – and it could eventually point to an increased gross profit margin on merchandise of 2.1%. Now that both teams had learned to align themselves and work together, the company's brand value was restored to the benefit of the bottom line.[2]

In 2015, Volkswagen found itself in trouble. A major scandal broke out when it was revealed that the company had installed software in its diesel vehicles to cheat emissions tests. Its "clean diesel" marketing campaign had been pushing the idea of environmentally friendly vehicles, while, during regular driving, its cars, in fact, emitted much higher levels of pollutants than claimed.

These are two very different cases: one a misstep at the strategy level, and the other a failure to curb the deeds of bad actors within the company who were showing disdain for the company's stated values. However, both cases serve as examples of the penalties that can be paid for lack of internal alignment.

The importance of including societal impact within the business case

In his bestselling book *Measure What Matters*,[3] as well as discussing the processes that made Intel successful, John Doerr outlines methods for using OKRs (Objectives and Key Results). OKRs have helped many firms, including Adobe and Google, accelerate growth and drive innovation by creating context and integrating their work into an overall company objective. The general idea is to set critical, publicly declared objectives for each team and to link them to crucial measurable parameters.

Google is one of the most well-known examples of companies that have enjoyed success with OKRs. Doerr introduced the OKR system to Google's leadership in the early 2000s with the aim of helping it maintain focus, prioritize strategic goals, and foster innovation. These OKRs played a crucial role in Google's rapid expansion and underpinned the successful launch of a range of products and services. (In Doerr's follow-up, *Speed & Scale*,[4] he brings OKRs to bear on a ten-step plan to achieve a state of global net-zero emissions by the year 2050, with a halfway mark to be attained by 2030.) Here is an example of how a company can use OKRs:

Objective: Drive Rapid Revenue Growth for [product]

Key Results:
- Roll out [product] feature to all users, ensuring widespread adoption.
- Execute [product] initiative to achieve a xx% increase in revenue per user.
- Conduct three revenue-focused experiments to gain insights into revenue growth drivers.
- Procure tech support to successfully develop [product] feature in Q1.

It is actually quite shocking to realize how few companies are setting "Purpose" objectives at a team or unit level or aligning group incentives to meet their "purpose" metrics. Again and again, we see teams making decisions that are not aligned with their firm's overall goals. Although, on the surface, OKRs may not always appear directly related to the firm's purpose, they will ultimately help team goals align with those of the firm. They help orient local teams in the direction of broader thinking that aligns with corporate purpose goals. In fact, when implemented correctly, they can change a firm's DNA. For example, to the "Key Results" section of the previous example, we could add:

- Ensure the product is carbon-neutral.
- Educate consumers on the true cost of energy.
- Reduce single-use plastic packaging by 15%.

By including societal impact in their return on investment (ROI) calculations, decision-making frameworks, and general metrics of success, managers can work toward transforming the company objective at a functional level. OKRs have proved their worth as a way for firms to develop new processes, improve dynamic capabilities, and harness objectives and opportunities.

When we incorporate "Purpose" into our financial calculations, such as return on investment (ROI), we gain full awareness of an action's true impact. A useful mindset in all business decision-making is to view the planet and society as stakeholders, just as you would customers, collaborators, and competitors. For example, a business case calculation might consider both environmental damage as well as financial impact on the local community. This is "stakeholder capitalism," and it proposes that businesses should not focus solely on maximizing profits for their shareholders but should also take into account the needs and concerns of other stakeholders, including, but not limited to, employees, customers, suppliers, communities, and the environment.

An optimal analysis of an opportunity will typically start with Porter's five forces: the bargaining power of suppliers, the bargaining power of buyers, the threat of new entrants, the threat of competition, and the threat of substitution.[5] Business schools teach this framework to budding new managers in the U.S. and across the world, as indeed do we in our own strategy classes: it's a starting point in evaluating a competitive opportunity and calculating the rate of return. A factor generally ignored, however, is the direct or indirect impact on the planet and people.

This is not to say that only those undertakings that are explicitly socially beneficial should be considered; what it does mean is that you should consider people and the planet from the moment you begin to evaluate an opportunity. *Will the firm's new enterprise make things better or worse for the environment? If an opportunity dramatically increases its carbon footprint, should a firm be investing in it? Will society benefit or lose from this?* These are the variables to be considered. If done so at the outset, managers will be making better decisions and aligning with broader corporate objectives. In the following sections, we will discuss how to quantify these metrics.

Impact-weighted accounting: the promise

You would not knowingly mistreat people or damage property, so why would you invest in products or stocks from a company that damages the environment or mistreats its employees? But how do you get the information to make such a value judgment?

Impact-weighted accounting is a promising new development that enables companies to report the financials alongside the impact of their activities worldwide. It offers transparency for ESG-related activities to allow companies to be evaluated on metrics other than the purely financial.

George Serafeim, a professor at Harvard Business School and author of the book *Purpose + Profit*, elaborates on this idea. According to his analysis, 15% of firms would be eliminated if environmental impacts were taken seriously.[6] Take American Airlines, for example. Based on Serafeim's research, the company would be unprofitable in a context where environmental and social impacts were openly reported and accounted for, owing to its substantial consumption of fuel and labor practices. Conversely, firms such as Intel, which offers employees unpaid leave and childcare support, would emerge more favorably. Few companies, however, report in this way. The leading French food corporation Danone, too, demonstrates a profit even after making adjustments to account for environmental damage.[7] Table 2.1

Table 2.1 Danone's goals and key performance indicators (KPIs)

Goal	KPIs
Make Danone a force for good by fostering a unique, diverse & inclusive culture and empowering Danoners for positive impact	All employees covered by B Corp certification by 2025
	All employees covered by Dan'Care by 2030
	Achieve gender balance in management globally by 2030
	Drive equity and close gender pay gap by 2025
	Maintain inclusion index above peers
Equip and empower communities (i.e. internal, external) with **skills and capabilities of the future** to thrive in a fast changing economy	Make future skilling programs available to all Danoners by 2025
	Extend future skilling programs to key partners by 2030
Champion a renewed social contract by fostering a prosperous & inclusive ecosystem, upholding human rights and pursuing social progress	100% employees trained on Danone Human Rights policy by 2025
	Danone Responsible Sourcing Policy deployed to all suppliers by 2030

Source: Danone Integrated Annual Report 2022. https://www.danone.com/integrated-annual-reports/integrated-annual-report-2022.html

shows how Danone developed its key objectives or key performance indicators (KPI) measurements.

However, for the majority of businesses, implementing impact-
weighted accounting would be like trying to run before they could
walk. There is still no such thing as a universal standard for calculating the true bottom line, nor is there unanimous agreement on
the measures to capture the three ESG categories. Without a complete integration of ESG into its internal functions, a company is
forced to retrofit the impact objectives. Only when such thinking is
brought to bear at the decision-making level can we talk of companies fully embracing pro-social strategies as part of their DNA. And
only then can effective Triple Bottom Line reporting follow; in fact,
it will come naturally as a result of holistic decision-making at the
unit level.

A framework for quantifying societal impact

To engage with this effectively, one simple approach is to include
the stakeholder impact as a separate item; in a more sophisticated
scenario, you can create multiple alternative versions of the calculations, using different societal and environmental impacts, such as
water saved, energy used, carbon, jobs created, brand equity,
improved Diversity, Equity, and Inclusion (DEI), etc. In this way,
the financial tradeoffs will be apparent, and a manager can see
whether there are any scenarios in which a product line (for example) can align with a company's values and be financially viable.
Here, pricing plays its part as a key variable.

Understand the value being created – for customers and society

We often get asked about ways to measure impact. This can be
complicated. Sometimes it involves multiple levels and subcate-
gories, with numbers inferred through assumptions and approxi-
mations.

Examples of the kind of calculations to be made are: how should
the savings accrued by a customer in using your product be incorporated into the calculations? One specific instance is the launch
of a washing machine that uses less water and the inclusion of
end-user water savings in the overall model impact calculation.
According to the U.S. Department of Energy, a regular full-sized
washing machine typically consumes 20 gallons of water per load.
In contrast, an Energy Star-certified washing machine, designed for
high efficiency, uses only 14 gallons of water per load, resulting in
a water saving of approximately 1,800 gallons per year. Using a

figure of $0.009 price per gallon, a consumer would save $162 a year by using Energy-Star machines. *The Strategy and Tactics of Pricing*[8] is a useful resource for an elaboration on this type of pricing model, explaining how companies can determine price based on value generated for the customer.

However, in today's context, this model is incomplete. It fails to represent the true price paid by all stakeholders as a result of your decision-making. A critical step is missing. Incorporating "true price" can lead a company to set prices and pitch their products differently. Below is the washing machine example again, with a simple calculation of value pricing, set out as a table:

Water savings per year	1,800 gallons (or $162)
Life of a washing machine	11 years
Gross customer lifetime savings	$1,782
Price difference between comparable water-efficient products	$100 (i.e. customers pay $100 more for the high-efficiency washing machine)
Net customer lifetime savings	$1,782 – $100 = $1,682

A typical pricing case analysis would end here (although the value savings would be communicated to the customer as part of marketing). This leads to two alternative scenarios:

Scenario 1: A buyer chooses a water-efficient washing machine; they sacrifice $100 in incremental price but save $1,682 in potential future water savings.

Scenario 2: A buyer chooses a more conventional washing machine; they save $100 upfront but sacrifice the potential $1,682.

Scenario 2 not only costs the customer more in the long run: it is also more environmentally harmful, wasting 1,800 gallons of clean water. It's relatively straightforward. But here's what happens when we add in the impact on planet and society, the "true cost."

First, there is the customer's water bill and then also the sewage bill – but these expenses may, in fact, account for only 25–50% of actual water-related costs. This is the case for manufacturing facilities. As well as basic household consumption water is also used for production and sanitation and by utilities. It undergoes various processes such as chemical treatment, heating, cooling, and filtration – and these all add to the cost of every single gallon, wherever it might end up. These processes – as well as the pumping costs – make each gallon much more expensive than originally assumed: maybe between two and four times the cost of the customer's water and sewage bills alone. For simplicity's sake, we will therefore say that water costs society three times as much as the amount the customer pays the water companies. The impact now looks like this:

$3 \times \$1,682 = \$5,046$ (the true cost of water)
Buyer pays $-\$1,682$
Cost to society $= \$3,364$

So, in essence, the Scenario 2 individual saved $100 in the short run, paid an extra $1,682 over the course of 11 years, and in the same period cost society $3,364. The decision to not purchase a high-efficiency washing machine was an individual one, based on the company's choice to charge a $100 premium for the product, which was an important lever for the customer's purchasing decision.

Equipped with knowledge of the true costs and social costs – and bearing in mind some customers' reluctance to pay an extra $100 – would managers make a different pricing judgment? A simple decision to lower the price by $100 to align with competitors could attract more customers and make more profit in the long run while also retaining strategic alignment with the firm's purpose-driven objectives.

The washing machine example will not necessarily end there: it could be expanded by adding in the cost of additional energy used to process 1,800 gallons of wastewater, for example. But we simply wanted to demonstrate the importance of understanding the impact of a single pricing decision on society and the environment.

Measurement challenges

Including social impact in your decision-making is not always quite so simple, and accurately quantifying the monetary impact of pro-social behaviors can be a challenge – especially in the current absence of measurement standards. In many cases, the benefits are only realizable in the long term, which makes it hard to account for them in a typical business case. Long, complicated calculations and a lack of unambiguous data can only lead to additional work. Our washing machine case was a simplified example, but it begins to hint at the level of complexity that can be involved.

However, the new business priorities we are witnessing have been accompanied by new data resources. Government regulations are pushing the needle on this, and as more and more firms report their Triple Bottom Line and engage in impact-weighted accounting, these types of calculations will soon become industry standard. Such big names as H&M, Patagonia, Walmart, and

Coca-Cola are already on board, having realized that their sustainability reports represent a good starting point for data and methodology that can assist in calculating the potential social impact of a product or service.

Measuring carbon emissions

Measuring the impact of a firm's carbon footprint is challenging. As a result, some companies fail to accurately present their true impact, which leads to misreporting and under-reporting of the damage caused.[9] In a report published by Boston Consulting Group in 2021, 81% of companies questioned failed to include certain internal emissions (i.e., those linked to the company's own operations), and 66% of respondents did not disclose any external emissions (those associated with the company's value chain). Respondents acknowledged an error rate of, on average, 30–40% in their emissions measurements.[10] To add to this complexity, assigning a financial number to a carbon footprint is, in fact, difficult: prone to assumptions and with wide margins of error. There are standardized metrics for certain aspects, like carbon emissions, but other metrics, such as the impact on fauna, water systems, climate, health, etc., may be broader-reaching and harder to quantify in monetary terms.

Companies can think about reducing carbon produced by activities and/or offsetting carbon produced by their activities. For example, investing in renewable energy sources to run the manufacturing operation would fall under the category of reducing carbon production. Alternatively, planting forests to recover the damage caused will fall under carbon offsetting activities. Carbon offsetting is a practice used to compensate for greenhouse gas emissions produced by human activities, such as driving a car, flying on an airplane, or operating a business, by investing in projects or activities that reduce or remove an equivalent amount of greenhouse gases from the atmosphere. The idea behind carbon offsetting is to achieve a net-zero carbon footprint, where the emissions generated are balanced out by the emissions reductions or removals elsewhere. Organizations calculate their carbon footprint by estimating the amount of greenhouse gases they emit through various activities, such as energy consumption, transportation, and manufacturing. This measurement is usually expressed in terms of carbon dioxide equivalent (CO_2eq) emissions. After determining their carbon footprint, individuals or organizations can purchase carbon offsets or carbon credits from projects and initiatives that are designed to reduce or remove an equivalent amount of greenhouse gases from the atmosphere. These projects can take various forms, including reforestation, afforestation, renewable energy installations (like wind or solar farms), methane capture at landfills, and energy efficiency programs. Put simply, companies calculate how many trees you would need to plant to offset the emissions and cost of production or carbon credits you need to purchase. *These costs included upfront when evaluating the business opportunity will provide the managers a view into the business's financial calculations.*

Being available on the open market, these credits are subject to market forces, and their value fluctuates accordingly (as of 2023, they stand at between $50 and $70 per metric ton). A 2021 *Harvard Business Review* article predicted the price of carbon to range between $50 and $100 per tonne in the short term.[11] Under the higher ($100) scenario, ExxonMobil would need to budget for $11 billion a year based on 2020 emissions. Firms such as Greenprint sell carbon credits to offset a company's carbon footprint. Additionally, the quality of carbon offset also dictates the price fluctuations based on permanence, leakage, etc., and benefits such as soil quality and community impacts.

However, carbon offsets do not always get good press, often being presented as being "used by polluters as a free pass for inaction."[12] Another issue is that emissions are typically offset in places where offsetting costs are lower, such as in emerging markets. It makes sense to buy these carbon credits from an economic point of view, but, in the words of *The Economist*, "some of these places would welcome investment in reforestation and afforestation, but they would also need to be able to integrate such endeavors into development plans which reflect their people's needs."[13] Here is a case in point. AKDN (Aga Khan Development Network) is an NGO that works with local communities in the poorest parts of Asia and Africa to alleviate poverty and improve the quality of life for the most vulnerable in society. Its mission also includes being a good steward of the environment. In northern Pakistan, for example, deforestation is a major problem, resulting in mudslides and negative local climatic effects. AKDN, therefore, planted several acres of trees. However, when they returned to the location several years later, they found that its trees had been cut down again; the locals had used the wood for cooking fires to feed their families. Understanding the local communities is an essential part of the tree-planting process, and understanding the social context is important in implementing sustained change. The next time around, when trees were planted, the community received efficient coal-burning stoves and was educated about the role trees play in preventing mudslides. We use this example to highlight that carbon offsetting, done right, is more than a cell on a spreadsheet, and companies should engage with and understand the implications of the offsetting projects they have chosen and the quality of carbon offsets purchased.

To build consumer awareness of the social costs, a grocery store in the Netherlands, De Aanzet, now sells its produce at two price points: regular price and true price. The regular price for tomatoes, for example, is €3.75 per kilo, whereas the true price, which accounts for hidden costs related to carbon emissions, worker underpayment along the supply chain, water, and land use, is €3.97 per kilo. This modest €0.22 difference reflects the additional expenses to society associated with growing and transporting the tomatoes, which are not captured in the regular price. Michel Scholte, co-founder of True Price, an organization dedicated to identifying and incorporating natural and social costs into market prices, said that he sees a 15–20% conversion to customers choosing to pay the higher price when both market price and true price are available for customers at purchase point. The additional funds captured from the price premium are used to improve soil quality and provide clean water, which impacts oxygen levels and the environment. In an experiment where only the true price was available, the researchers saw a 95% conversion.

Measuring a life saved

Putting a price on human life and health is a sensitive topic. However, the insurance industry has already been doing this for a long time, and in the U.S., actuarial science has developed ways of quantifying a range of social issues, including interesting and creative ways of assigning numbers to the value of a person's life. However, this topic will never be less than contentious. Consider how it played out during the pandemic: governments were forced to evaluate the tradeoffs between keeping the economy running or shutting it down to save lives.

To evaluate the best time to open the economy, governments during the pandemic drew on the work of Betsy Stevenson, an economist from the University of Michigan. Stevenson's work does indeed calculate the statistical monetary value of human life by taking the amounts that people invest in safety and the extra that someone would be paid for doing a dangerous job. Her research concluded that the current value of a human life is $3 million.[14] This number was the key metric in determining whether the lockdown should continue or not. However controversial or unfeeling these kinds of metrics might seem, they can prove crucial in assigning numbers to an otherwise nebulous decision.

Measuring jobs created or lost

Another measure that can be used is job creation and what it adds to a region's economic stability. Accounting firms are now getting heavily involved in employee metrics from an ESG perspective and calculating the numbers of jobs saved or impacted. Such numbers will vary by region, but there are basically three things to consider: an individual's increased income, increased income tax for the government, and (in some cases) a decrease in social assistance payments.

In 2013, Dutch chocolate company Tony's Chocolonely embarked on a comprehensive calculation of the costs associated with cocoa production in Ghana and the Ivory Coast. The assessment included eight environmental externalities, including pollution and climate change, and six social factors, including insufficient income and child labor. These regions, which supply most of the world's cocoa, have long-standing issues with labor practices involving children. The average true cost of cocoa per kilogram was calculated at €14.17, with the majority (€12.07) attributed to social externalities. Tony's Chocolonely was committed to improving its sourcing practices and managed to reduce its average true cost to a significantly lower €7.93, of which €5.99 were social costs. When the company commissioned another study in 2017, the true price had further reduced to €4.52, with €2.93 as social costs. This was confirmation that its endeavors to reduce its impact across the supply chain had been successful. While these costs are only estimates, Tony's Chocolonely nonetheless found them valuable in setting goals and tracking progress in its initiatives. Today, the company can boast a tenfold revenue growth over ten years, increasing its gross margins from approximately 42% to 46%.

The social cost of food

In a 2021 study by the Rockefeller Foundation,[15] it was found that the true social cost of food in the U.S. has to account for the damage done to the environment through the transportation of food, low wages paid to children, and health outcomes as a result of chemical use. The study confirms that the true price of produce is as much as three times the price we pay in the grocery store. Figure 2.1 elaborates on the impact across areas of biodiversity, livelihood, human health, economy, and environment (see Figure 2.1).

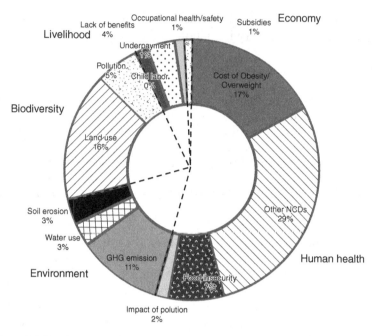

Figure 2.1 True costs: quantitative metrics across multiple impact areas.

Other measurements

We have looked at ways to assign numbers to lives saved, jobs created, and carbon emissions. Other impacts, such as water and energy, are easier to calculate.

True costs and responsible business: getting there

Firms and the communities in which they operate now appreciate that a shift to calculating true costs requires a long-term outlook. Based on this, we can calibrate the equation for calculating purpose-driven pricing, as shown in Figure 2.2. In the short term, firms should focus on being ESG-compliant, and seek to meet the needs of all their stakeholders: customers, employees, suppliers, collaborators, communities, and the planet. As a firm embarks on this opportunity analysis, the most important step is to begin accounting for the impacts caused by new product introduction. As a firm matures on its journey, it can include the impact made by the firm as a whole, as well as those of its suppliers and collaborators. We understand that this has broad implications, not least being the time-consuming nature of the calculations. We advise firms to start

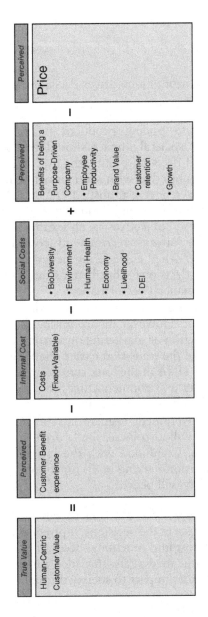

Figure 2.2 Purpose-driven pricing equation.

with immediate internal alignment, using a system that engages with the overall goal of changing its DNA, which means learning to see its impact on society and the financial implications associated with this transformation and incorporating of "Purpose" thinking into everyday decision-making at a unit level.

Key takeaways

Focusing on financial profit alone drives decisions that can oppose a firm's "Purpose" goals.

- When designing and pricing products, financial targets are important, but the societal impact should be considered and evaluated. So, at all decision points, the first step should be to align your project objective with your firm's "Purpose." Many companies these days have established "Purpose" as a guiding principle and will develop their products and services around it. Retrofitting "Purpose" objectives in an established company is challenging, so we always recommend considering societal impact at the outset when considering new opportunities. This will drive different decisions – but better ones, both for society and for the firm's financial performance.
- Calculating the monetary impact of purpose-driven activities is a complex undertaking. However, incorporating them in the evaluation of new production or marketing opportunities is the way to begin and will make the transition easier, enabling "Purpose" to penetrate the firm's DNA in the long run. We've discussed incorporating social costs (environment, life, food, jobs) and adding these costs in to the financial evaluations.
- External forces (government regulation, consumers, investors, and collaborators) will also increasingly drive companies faster toward these goals. Combined with the internal alignment of purpose-driven decision-making in all functional areas, both the company and society will benefit.

The focus of this chapter was for firms to seek internal alignment and understand true costs of the decisions. It provides managers with ways to capture true cost into functional decision-making. In subsequent chapters, we will investigate this idea further and look at incorporating the broader impact to society through a pricing lens.

Notes

1 Herman Aguinis and Ante Glavas, "Embedded versus Peripheral Corporate Social Responsibility: Psychological Foundations." *Industrial*

and Organizational Psychology 6(4) (December 2013): 314–332. https://doi.org/10.1111/iops.12059

Kunal Basu and Guido Palazzo, "Corporate Social Responsibility: A Process Model of Sensemaking." *Academy of Management Review* 33(1) (January 2008): 122–136. https://www.jstor.org/stable/20159379

Simon Brooks, "Corporate Social Responsibility and Strategic Management: The Prospects for Converging Discourses." *Strategic Change* 14(7) (November 2005): 401–411. https://doi.org/10.1002/jsc.731

2 Phil Wahba, "Why Ralph Lauren's Plan to Ditch Discounts Is Paying Off." *Fortune*, August 8, 2017. https://fortune.com/2017/08/08/ralph-lauren-luxury/

3 John Doerr, *Measure What Matters: How Google, Bono, and the Gates Foundation Rock the World with OKRs* (Portfolio, 2018).

4 John Doerr, *Speed & Scale: A Global Action Plan for Solving Our Climate Crisis Now* (Penguin, 2021).

5 Michael E. Porter, "How Competitive Forces Shape Strategy." *Harvard Business Review* 57(2) (May 1979): 137–145.

6 George Serafeim, *Purpose + Profit: How Business Can Lift Up the World* (HarperCollins Leadership, 2022).

7 Danone Integrated Annual Report 2022. https://www.danone.com/integrated-annual-reports/integrated-annual-report-2022.html

8 Thomas T. Nagle, John Hogan, and Joseph Zale, *The Strategy and Tactics of Pricing* (5th edn; Routledge, 2016).

9 Robert S. Kaplan and Karthik Ramanna, "We Need Better Carbon Accounting: Here's How to Get There." *Harvard Business Review*, April 12, 2022. https://hbr.org/2022/04/we-need-better-carbon-accounting-heres-how-to-get-there

10 BCG, "New BCG GAMMA Survey Reveals That Only 9% of Organizations Are Able to Measure Their Total Greenhouse Gas Emissions Comprehensively." Press Release, October 13, 2021. https://www.bcg.com/press/13october2021-only-nine-percent-of-organizations-measure-emissions-comprehensively

11 Robert G. Eccles and John Mulliken, "Carbon Might Be Your Company's Biggest Financial Liability." *Harvard Business Review*, October 7, 2021. https://hbr.org/2021/10/carbon-might-be-your-companys-biggest-financial-liability

12 United Nations Environment Programme, "Letter from the Executive Director: 2019 in Review." https://www.unep.org/annualreport/2019/index.php

13 "The Necessity of Pulling Carbon Dioxide out of the Air." *The Economist*, December 7, 2019. https://www.economist.com/leaders/2019/12/07/the-necessity-of-pulling-carbon-dioxide-out-of-the-air

14 NPR, "Lives vs. the Economy." Planet Money, April 15, 2020. https://www.npr.org/transcripts/835571843

15 The Rockefeller Foundation, *True Cost of Food: Measuring What Matters to Transform the U.S. Food System* (July 2021). https://www.rockefellerfoundation.org/wp-content/uploads/2021/07/True-Cost-of-Food-Full-Report-Final.pdf

3 Innovation diffusion
Pricing for growth

> Just like a good leader, innovation must improve society and not harm it.
>
> Anonymous

In this chapter, we will discuss monetization models and pricing strategies that help accelerate the adoption of purpose-driven products and services at different stages of diffusion. The diffusion process can be influenced by various factors, such as the characteristics of the innovation itself, the communication channels used to promote it, the characteristics of the adopters, and the macroeconomic and social context in which the innovation is introduced. By understanding this process, innovators can better plan and implement strategies to increase the likelihood of successful adoption and spread of their innovations. In this chapter, we explore the influence of price on each stage of diffusion.

The "diffusion of innovation" stages and the role of pricing

Innovation diffusion is the process by which new ideas, products, technologies, or practices spread throughout a population or social system over time. It refers to how individuals or organizations communicate, adapt, and accept innovation. Everett Rogers[1] developed a theory in 1962 to explain how and why innovations are adopted and spread. According to this "diffusion of innovation" theory, the diffusion process can be described as a series of five stages: Innovators, Early Adopters, Early Majority, Late Majority, and Laggards.

But pricing can also represent a challenge for innovation, especially when companies have low certainty about market demand, the competitive landscape, or the cost structure of the new product or service. This chapter will explore innovation and how companies can balance value creation, monetize innovation, and increase customers' propensity for purpose-driven behavior using pricing.

Monetization models are critical, being particularly relevant to profitability and the long-term viability of an innovation.

DOI: 10.4324/9781032659008-4

Here is a important to define monetization. Monetization entails crafting an offer framework that transforms non-revenue-generating assets into revenue streams. Effective monetization strategies allow companies to capture the total value of their innovations; poor monetization decisions lead to missed revenue opportunities and even business failure. We want products and services that are good for society to be successful and widely adopted. Traditional monetization models involve just a single exchange: a customer buys the product at a certain price; the firm's revenue is calculated based on price and volume received from the customer base. However, in contemporary markets, a firm can have multiple revenue streams by finding ways to moneize other aspects of the business such as data. Instacart, for example, a web grocer in the U.S., has multiple revenue streams, among them:

1. Customers pay a service and delivery fee or membership subscription.
2. Instacart marks up the groceries.
3. The partners (Kroger, CostCo, etc.) pay fees.
4. Manufacturers pay to advertise on Instacart's website or mobile app.

Instacart can use a different pricing model for each revenue stream and, additionally, it doesn't depend solely on its customers for revenue. Monetization-model decisions have important implications for the pricing model, costs, and profitability. When monetization strategies are misaligned, products can fail. Here are some examples:

- Apple Lisa (1983). The Apple Lisa was one of the first personal computers with a graphical user interface – a revolutionary piece of technology that would become a staple of modern computing – but it was priced at $9,995, far beyond what most consumers were willing to pay, despite its cutting-edge technology. As a result, it sold poorly and was eventually discontinued.[2]
- MoviePass (2019). Founded in 2011, MoviePass introduced the idea of allowing people to purchase movie theater tickets on a mobile app. In 2017, the company rolled out a new plan: a monthly subscription of $9.95, enabling customers to watch unlimited movies at a theater. In 2018, it dropped the price to $7.95 and then to $6.95. Soon, they had nearly three million members. However, the product was priced too low, and the unit cost economics did not work. The theaters were charging MoviePass full price more to buy these movie tickets for their subscribers, which was $10–14 per movie. The plan to monetize data to supplement the customer revenue stream never really took off. Hence, despite its considerable customer base, MoviePass closed in 2019.[3]

Monetization and pricing strategies are critical for innovation because, by determining the value of a new product or service to customers and the revenue a company can generate, they can drive innovation by incentivizing companies to invest in research and development and in shaping customer behavior.

It's hard to overemphasize the importance of pricing in the success of an innovation and its monetization process: it has a direct bearing on the commercial success of new products, services, and business models. At this point, it's worth looking at some traditional pricing strategies that can be brought to bear on the challenges of pricing in innovation:

- **Penetration pricing.** Entering the market at a low price with the aim of rapidly capturing a large market share.
- **Price skimming.** The firm prices at a premium, aiming to swiftly recoup costs related to product manufacturing and promotion. It may drop the price subsequently, having "skimmed" the layer of customers who were willing to pay the high price. The primary goal is to achieve high profits rapidly. Businesses frequently resort to price skimming when they are in their initial stages and need financial resources.
- **Value-based pricing.** Determining the price of a product according to the perceived value attributed to it by the customer.
- **Competitor-based pricing.** Setting product prices in accordance with the pricing of competing products, as opposed to focusing on cost or target profit, often results in prices lower than those of competitors.
- **Cost-plus pricing.** Applying a consistent percentage increase to the production cost of a product, irrespective of consumer demand or the pricing strategies of competitors. A variation of cost-plus pricing is *target costing*, a strategy often used by Japanese firms. This involves estimating the target cost for a product based on the price that customers are willing to pay. Instead of starting with the cost of production and adding a profit margin (as in traditional cost-plus pricing), target costing begins with the market price and subtracts the desired profit margin, leaving the costs of production within which the company must work.

Pricing of innovations and its influence on societal welfare

An effective pricing strategy will capture both the total value of the innovation created for customers and society. Ignoring the "social cost," discussed in the previous chapter, can lead to undervaluing

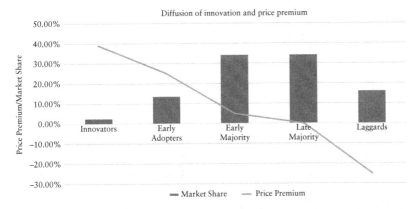

Figure 3.1 Five stages of innovation adoption and corresponding price premium for pro-social products over conventional products.

Source: Adapted from Everett M. Rogers, *Diffusion of Innovations* (The Free Press, 1962).

the broader societal implications of the innovation. Recall the stages of diffusion of innovation discussed earlier (see Figure 3.1). We can now look at how pricing affects social welfare at various stages in that journey.

Stage 1: Innovators (2.5% market share)

These individuals are eager to be the first to embrace innovation. They possess a spirit of adventure and a fascination with novel concepts. They readily take risks and often lead the charge in developing groundbreaking ideas. Little to no persuasion is required to engage this demographic. Innovators are the first group of users to adopt a new product. They are typically a tiny but critical market segment willing to take risks and experiment with new products. They are hobby enthusiasts and risk-takers. At this stage, a manager's mind will usually be occupied by considerations of product design, monetization strategy, and establishing product–market fit. The innovative aspect might be the product's design, the supply chain, monetization models, raw materials, and so on. In this stage, we find the companies would be best served to focus on the segment of customers who value the "purpose" benefits and are willing to pay more.

Corporate purpose has stimulated managers to think outside the box and find new and creative ways of addressing societal concerns while also being profitable. In the case of Discovery Health (see Box) in South Africa was concerned with doing good from the outset, so the innovation here is the business model itself and how the firm measures and prices its services. Innovations can be in products, services, or changes in the monetization or business model itself which can generate value for customers and society.

Case: Discovery

Discovery is an insurance provider based in South Africa with an innovative business model that incentivizes people to live healthier lives. It encourages its customers to go to the gym, for example, or eat a more nutritious diet, through pricing – by providing discounts and rebates.

Founder Adrian Gore came upon this idea when working as an actuarial analyst. Smoking, poor nutrition, and poor physical health are critical drivers of non-communicable diseases such as diabetes, cancer, and heart and lung disease – which are responsible for over 50% of mortality. Lifestyle is, therefore, fundamental to good health outcomes and, as a result, lower insurance costs. The numbers make sense economically as well.

Members have about 30% fewer hospitalizations and live between 13 and 21 years longer than those using other insurance services.[4] The firm has accomplished this by using price as a lever via the price discounts that reward good behavior. The shared value created higher profits for Discovery and better health for its customers and costs of healthcare from a society viewpoint.

Stage 2: Early adopters (13.5% market share)

These are the trendsetters and opinion shapers. They thrive in leadership roles and readily seize opportunities for change. They are already attuned to the need for change, making them comfortable adopting new ideas. Strategies to engage this group should involve providing practical guides and implementation resources, as they require no persuasion. At this stage, a company focuses on enhancing the product's perceived value and acceptability rather than maximizing profits – which can be achieved by offering the product at a premium price, thereby implying its uniqueness and exclusivity. The pricing typically reflects the costs of development and the product's value proposition.

The Early Adopters follow on from the previous group, the Innovators, and typically represent a larger market segment. They are more risk-averse than Innovators but still willing to try new products. At this stage, the pricing strategy should focus on leveraging the momentum generated by the Innovators to maximize trial, create value and experience, and establish the product.

Firms at Stage 2 can often be seen launching new products at a premium price. Market share at this stage is typically less than 20%, and economies of scale are minimal. The percent of price premium varies based on the product category, on average, ranging from (20–50%) of the conventional product.

The "green premium"

As we discussed in Chapter 1, consumers have become more environmentally conscious since as far back as the 1970s, leading to the development and publication of ESG standards in the 1980s. Companies responded by introducing eco-friendly products – an excellent opportunity to differentiate the product line and charge more – the "green premium" or green tax. According to NYU's sustainability index, eco-friendly products are priced approximately 27% higher than conventional alternatives. Although the market share of these products has grown, the price premium has stayed above 25% over the last five years, and, furthermore, it does not vary much by product category (see Figure 3.2). Studies repeatedly find that many customers are willing to pay this premium (see Chapter 1).

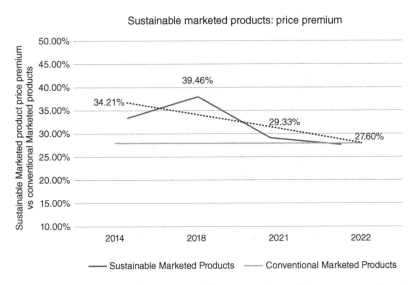

Figure 3.2 Price premium for sustainably marketed products vs. conventional products.

Source: Adapted from Randi Kronthal-Sacco and Tensie Whelan, "Sustainable Market Share Index: 2021 Report." NYU Stern Center for Sustainable Business, April 2022. https://www.stern.nyu.edu/sites/default/files/assets/documents/FINAL%20 2021%20CSB%20Practice%20Forum%20website_0.pdf

Companies have different motivations for charging this premium.

• Some of the price premium is driven by a motivation to *recover the initial investment in research* and commercialization of these innovations.
• Companies seek to *maximize profit* by exploiting this consumer segment's willingness to pay more for eco-products.[5] However, the price often stays high simply because of the *minimum* profitability needed (as per the first point).
• Companies also appreciate that this segment's willingness to pay means that they are receptive to the enhanced *quality perception* conferred by the higher price. (In the next chapter, we will discuss consumer behavior in relation to quality–price connections.)
• Price differentiates the products from the companies' conventional product line. The higher price point has sometimes followed as a response to the "cannibalization" of conventional products with green products.
• There are higher raw materials and supply chain costs – which can also mean higher manufacturing and distribution costs – to recoup. Recyclable packaging, for example, can cost more. As Freya Williams has noted, "One of the biggest sticking points for many companies seeking to drive sustainability responsibility deep into the business is cost."[6] Although sustainable practices such as energy efficiency save money, some can push costs up. Retrofitting businesses to accommodate these additional costs is challenging, Williams notes. In the long run, sustainability may work out in the firm's favor, but, in the short run, they are stuck with the choice of either absorbing these costs or passing them on to the consumer. A few companies, such as Chipotle and Nissan, with its Leaf model, have successfully launched reasonably priced products by building a business model around these costs rather than retrofitting them onto existing products.

Stage 3: Early majority (34% market share)

The Early Majority represents the tipping point for the diffusion of innovation. This group of users is larger and more skeptical than the Early Adopters, and they need more convincing. While not typically leaders, these individuals are early to adopt new ideas ahead of the general population. However, they usually seek evidence of an innovation's effectiveness before embracing it. Strategies to attract this segment should emphasize success stories and concrete proof of the innovation's impact. The pricing strategy at this stage should focus on making the product more affordable and accessible to this group of users. The pricing should reflect the lower production costs and economies of scale achieved by mass production.

In a study published in February 2023, McKinsey and NeilsonQ[7] analyzed five years of transaction data from 2017 to 2022. The study covered 600,000 products sold in the U.S., making over $400 billion in yearly sales. Products comprised 44,000 brands across personal care, food, beverages, and household categories. The study noted that products making purpose-related claims averaged 28% cumulative growth over the previous five years compared to 20% for products that made no such claims.

One of the key recommendations from the study relates to the product design process. It encourages companies to ensure that the *cost of producing products* should be considered in the product's design, and cost efficiency for sustainable products should be maximized. Currently, purpose claims serve as a value driver for a firm, i.e., specific customer segments are willing to pay more. However, as more competition enters the market, price competition intensifies to preserve/gain market share. The lower costs will enable the firm to stay competitive and price lower stay competitive.

Case of Tesla

For a while, Tesla was the only luxury electric vehicle available, so customers had no other option and would pay a premium. Tesla charged a premium price over and above the monetary benefits and savings generated for fuel purchases. More recently, however, as more players entered the industry, customers have other options, including BMW, Mercedes Benz, and Audi, who are all developing electric versions of their cars. So, in 2022–23, Tesla reduced the prices of several of its models by as much as 20%, with the most significant discounts being for the more affordable product lines, further enhancing their affordability.[8] However, this model included decreased manufacturing costs, pushing Tesla into the next stage.

Case: McDonald's salads

When in 2013 McDonald's first launched a salad as a healthier option, it failed disastrously.

Because fast-food chains have significant customers from lower-income populations, who have poorer health outcomes, they are under fire for being part of the problem. Under pressure to offer nutritious options, McDonald's wanted a salad on its menu to be seen to be doing something to combat the U.S.'s obesity epidemic. However, when it launched, no one bought it! The salads were priced higher than the ever-popular burgers: with a Big Mac at $4.19, the Southwest Chicken Salad's $4.89 represented a price premium of 15% and, furthermore, wasn't perceived as satisfying your hunger to the same extent. McDonald's rolled out the salads across the nation, making its healthy option widely available. The marketing campaign increased awareness and also communicated its health benefits. So, it fulfilled the "availability" criterion; what it didn't do was create "acceptability" and repurchase intent.[9]

The failure of the McDonald's salad brings up an important point about Corporate Social Responsibility. Did McDonald's fulfill its social obligations by offering a healthier option on its menu? Or should it have gone a step further and ensured it was more acceptable to customers in order to incentivize them into buying it? In 2023, you no longer see any healthy choices on a McDonald's menu; look in vain for salad, grilled chicken sandwich, or yogurt parfait!

Stage 4: Late majority (34% market share)

Crossing the chasm: Driving adoption and market share (34%)

The next group of users to adopt a new product is what is termed the Late Majority. They are typically a more significant market segment than the Early Majority but also more conservative and risk averse. This group tends to be skeptical of change and only adopts innovations once they are widely accepted. To appeal to them, provide information about the widespread adoption and successful experiences of others who have embraced the innovation. The strategy at this stage should focus on maximizing market penetration, which means lowering the product's price.

So, although the decision to charge a price premium is plausible in the initial stages and, in many cases, necessary. However, in the case of many eco-friendly products, many firms have gotten comfortable with getting the price premium and the higher profits that come with it and have not progressed to driving wider adoption by lowering prices. In many cases, such as electronics, we can observe the "price skimming" strategy discussed above, where the product is initially introduced at a higher price. As product adoption grows, the price steadily comes down. We've seen this in the cases of flat-screen televisions, VCRs, cell phones, etc. So why is this not happening when it comes to eco-friendly products?

The market share for eco-friendly products has remained steady at 20%, but we're still waiting for mass adoption, as we can observe with other innovations. Freya Williams has noted that "price is a primary factor preventing the mass adoption of eco-friendly products." Environmental awareness will not lead to major change if it remains just a fad of the wealthy as long as mass adoption is priced out. Managers, of course, have perennially faced the dilemma of balancing market share and profitability. Massive players like Amazon and Meta have become the behemoths they are by focusing on market share in their initial years, forgoing profit in the process. This kind of strategy, focusing on market share and staying relevant, is becoming increasingly common. Once again, price is the key lever, to be tweaked to favor market share over profitability and vice versa. Pricing decisions are pivotal, as they impact the adoption and market share of new products or services; a price point perceived as too high or too low makes all the difference, driving consumer behavior, including that which is either purpose-driven or otherwise.

As companies progress along the stages of diffusion, in the later stages, pricing strategies should be focused on driving growth and mass adoption of products and services that are good for society and increasing prices for products that do not produce positive social outcomes.

Georgia-Pacific Case Study

Georgia-Pacific is a leading American pulp and paper company with a diverse product portfolio encompassing paper products, building materials, and packaging solutions. Known for its commitment to sustainability, the company operates with a focus on responsible forestry practices and environmental stewardship. A subsidiary of Koch Industries, Georgia-Pacific plays a significant role in the forest products industry and is recognized for brands such as "Brawny" and "Angel Soft" in the consumer products sector. The firm is expanding from environmentally conscious consumer segments – and their willingness-to-pay – and exploring other segments; as such, prices will need to go down to capture these new segments. Prices need to be reduced quickly in the last of our two diffusion of innovation stages in order to encourage adoption, achieve economies of scale, and transition to a broader take-up of environmentally preferable products. Much of the initial R&D cost is likely to have been recovered by this stage, so the company can still aspire to a reasonable margin profit even while focusing on market penetration. We discuss this case in greater depth in Chapter 9.

Stage 5: Laggards (16% market share)

Laggards is the name given to the final group of users to adopt a new product, and it comprises approximately 16% of total customers. This is typically a small and conservative market segment. Rooted in tradition and deeply conservative, laggards are the most resistant to change. Winning them over requires employing statistics, fear-based appeals, and peer pressure from those in other adopter groups. The pricing strategy at this stage should focus on liquidating inventory and maximizing profits by means of discounts and promotions. Alternatively, the pricing for established products, can reflect the need to move the product out of the market and make room for new products. By discouraging the use of products that are not good for society and instead incentivizing the purchase of new products that improve society. Managing the price gap between new and old products – using the behavioral techniques discussed in the next chapter – customers can be encouraged to trade up and shift purchase behavior. As companies continue to innovate, replacing old technogy with newer, better products is imporant.

The following sections discuss innovations in cleaning products, light bulbs, and water bottles. These discussions are located in the latter stages (4 and 5). In these cases, we propose different pricing strategies for each, based on their environmental impacts.

Accelerate take-up of purposeful products with affordable prices

CASE: LED BULBS

LED bulbs represent a revolution in the lighting industry. LEDs (light-emitting diodes) convert electricity into light by means of a semiconductor but without the wire filaments of traditional incandescent bulbs; they produce more brightness with less energy and last longer. The story of their innovation goes back to the early 1960s when a scientist named Nick Holonyak Jr. invented a laser diode that was the forerunner of the LED. However, it wasn't until the 1990s that LED technology improved to the point where it was sufficiently cheap and efficient for commercial use. This was when General Electric, Philips, and Cree began manufacturing LED bulbs for traffic lights and other niche applications.

LED bulbs have several advantages over traditional incandescent bulbs and also over the much newer fluorescent bulbs.

The first is *energy efficiency*: they use up to 85% less energy than conventional bulbs and produce less heat. Secondly, they are *longer-lasting*: LED bulbs can last up to 25 times longer than incandescent bulbs. The third advantage is their *versatility*: LEDs can be used in a range of lighting applications, including indoor and outdoor and accent lighting. They are also available in multiple colors, including warm white, cool white, and daylight, allowing for customization and flexibility. Finally, one of their key properties is the ability to produce *high-quality light*. LED bulbs produce light very close in color temperature to natural sunlight, making them ideal for use in spaces where natural light is limited or non-existent. LED bulbs can also produce various color temperatures, making them suitable for multiple lighting applications.

In the early 2000s, the technology continued to improve, and LED bulbs began to enter the mainstream market. However, these early LED bulbs were still relatively expensive and still not as efficient as they are today. A critical innovation came in 2008 when a company called Bridgelux introduced a more efficient LED chip, which allowed the bulbs to produce more light with less energy, making them more cost-effective and practical for widespread use. In the following years, other companies continued to innovate and improve LED bulb technology. For example, in 2013, Cree introduced a new type that could produce over 1,600 lumens with just 23 watts of energy – a significant improvement that further boosted their popularity[10]. LED bulbs have had a profound impact on the way we light our homes and businesses, as well as on energy consumption.

LED bulb technology has continued to evolve, with manufacturers constantly improving their efficiency and performance. New and innovative products continue to emerge, such as smartphone apps to control the lights, allowing users to adjust the color temperature and brightness of their lighting and set schedules and timers.

PRICING STRATEGY

Notwithstanding all their advantages, LED bulbs are currently *two to three times* the price of an incandescent bulb. A standard 60-watt incandescent bulb may cost around $2–3, while an equivalent LED bulb is priced at around $5–7. A price disparity of this size significantly slows down the adoption rate. The adoption of LED bulbs in the U.S. is 50–60%, but the global market share is lower. A study by Fortune Business Insights noted that "The global LED lighting market is projected to grow from $85.02 billion in 2022 to $264.08 billion by 2029, at a CAGR of 17.6% in the forecast period, 2022–2029"[11] (see Figure 3.3). It continued to note that

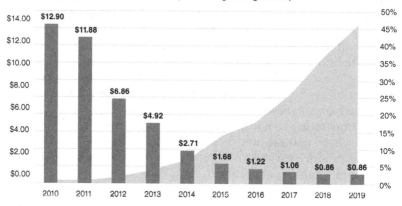

LED lighting costs decline as volumes increase
(US$ cost per kilolumen / LEDs as a percent of global lights sold)

Figure 3.3 US$ per kilolumen/global sales are shown as costs decline and LED sales increase.

Source: US Department of Energy and International Energy Agency. https://www.freeingenergy.com/facts/led-bulb-light-cost-price-historical-decline-g213

"the high initial costs of deployment costs restrain market share growth globally." If the use of LED bulbs is to be encouraged, they should be *priced lower* than regular bulbs or, at a minimum, at an equivalent price. If the current pricing strategy – which currently requires the buyer to lay out an initial higher cost even if lifetime cost savings will accrue – is going to be maintained, then behavioral pricing strategies could be used to encourage adoption by creating a power price perception. These strategies might revolve around packaging, size, bundling, etc. Incentives can also play a part, such as tax rebates or subsidies. Manufacturers can push the transition by producing fewer regular lighting products SKUs, and retailers can dedicate more shelf space to LED lights. Regulations and mandates can also play an important role in adoption, as seen in Australia among other places. In Australia, Minimum Energy Performance Standards (MEPS) have set requirements for energy-efficient lighting products. Rebates and incentives through the Energy Savings Scheme (ESS) have further propelled the transition.

Maintaining or increasing prices of non-purpose-driven products and services in the later stages

CASE: PLASTIC BOTTLES

Slowing the growth of environmentally damaging products

According to a recent report, the global bottled water industry is thriving, with over 1 million bottles of water being sold every minute worldwide. Furthermore, the industry is projected to maintain its rapid growth: global bottled water sales are estimated to almost double by 2030. The 2023 report, published by the United Nations University Institute for Water, Environment and Health, points to the tremendous global success of the bottled water industry.[12] But it's a prosperity that comes at a significant price, as the report underscores, considering the industry's substantial environmental, climate, and social impacts. In 2021 alone, around 600 billion plastic bottles were generated,[13] contributing to approximately 25 million tons of plastic waste not being recycled and going into landfills. There is so much of this trash, the report noted, that it could fill a line of 40-ton trucks stretching end-to-end from New York to Bangkok *every year*. Plastics made from fossil fuels carry a substantial carbon footprint from production to disposal; they have been labeled "climate killers." If the plastics industry were a country, it would rank as the fifth-largest greenhouse gas emitter worldwide.

In the U.S., the recycling rate for plastic bottles is around 30%; in the U.K., somewhere between 20% and 45%. Worldwide, however, about 85% of plastic water bottles end up as waste. Many become litter in natural environments such as rivers, oceans, and forests, which harms wildlife and their ecosystems, ending up being ingested or entangling them. The bottles that find their way into the ocean pose a grave threat to marine life. Plastic water bottles take hundreds of years to degrade fully. Instead, in the short term, they break down into smaller and smaller pieces and eventually turn into "microplastics," which can contaminate food and water sources, potentially affecting human health and entering food chains. Moreover, as they degrade, the plastic can leach toxic chemicals, including bisphenol-A (BPA) and phthalates, which can also infiltrate food chains.

The low price of plastic water bottles – as well as their general availability and convenience – have contributed to their widespread use and casual disposal. The low cost of production and materials is a major factor here, too, notwithstanding the significant amounts of energy and resources, such as oil and water, required in plastic bottle production, further adding to greenhouse gas emissions.

So, how can businesses address this issue and seek to reduce consumption? By *increasing the price of plastic bottles*. That's right: increase the price. This will inevitably lead to reduced use and hopefully encourage people to carry reusable bottles. Increased prices will reduce volume sales, but the profits remain stable reduced consumption is, however, better for the environment. Although this strategy seems challenging in the American system with a consumerism mindset and price wars, a proactive approach by corporations will prevent legislation and policy action.

The other challenge is that the entire industry has to come together to increase prices, which has legal issues of collusion. Alternatively, governments can impose taxes similar to those on nicotine products – in this case, corporations will lose the additional revenue from the increased prices to the government in the form of taxes. Chapter 5 discusses more governmental strategies in this vein of incentivizing behaviors.

In many countries, however, bottled water is an essential purchase because of the lack of safe drinking water. A two-pronged strategy is needed in such areas (alongside any increase in the price of plastic bottles): increase the availability of safe drinking water and distribute reusable bottles. Not just in these areas but worldwide, there is a strong case for encouraging the use of reusable water bottles – which can be achieved with lower prices and wider availability. Incentives, such as discounts or loyalty points, can be offered for bringing such bottles can be offered for refill at water dispensers or stations.

A study conducted by Holidu[14] found that Oslo has the highest-priced bottled water in the world at $1.80 versus $0.75 in Stockholm and $0.55 in Atlanta. Norway has used an exciting pricing strategy to increase the recycling of plastic water bottles, and its efficient and environmentally friendly scheme has achieved remarkable success. With an organization called Infinitum leading the way, Norway has managed to recycle an impressive 97% of all plastic bottles used, with less than 1% ending up in the environment. Even more impressive is that 92% of the recycled bottles yield high-quality material that can be reused for other drink bottles, sometimes more than 50 times.

Norway's success lies in giving recycling a financial value. Consumers pay a small additional fee – about ¢13–30 – when buying a plastic bottle, which can be redeemed through "reverse vending machines" or returned to small shops and gas stations for cash or store credit. This financial incentive has proven effective, motivating companies and consumers to take the proper environmental steps and promoting a circular economy where packaging is treated as a borrowed resource. This achievement stands out while the world is struggling with its recycling plastic waste: only 9% of global plastic production is recycled, and 8 million metric tons end up in the ocean annually.

In California, consumers are charged a California Redemption Value (CRV) fee when they buy beverages. They can recoup this fee by returning containers to a participating recycling center or retailer, known within the program as "dealers." The majority of beverages eligible for CRV come in containers made of either aluminum, glass, plastic, or bimetal. The CRV refund rates vary: 5 cents for containers with a capacity of less than 24 ounces, 10 cents for containers weighing 24 ounces or larger, and 25 cents for wine or distilled spirits enclosed in a box, bladder, pouch, or similar container. Starting from January 1, 2024, all types of wine and distilled spirit containers will be included in the program.

Finding creative alternatives

CASE: THE KEURIG COFFEE MAKER

The Keurig coffee maker was invented in the early 1990s by John Sylvan,[15] who was frustrated with the time and hassle involved in making a single cup of coffee using traditional methods. Sylvan saw an opportunity to create a more convenient and efficient coffee-making device to brew a single cup of coffee quickly and easily.

Sylvan founded Keurig, Inc. in 1992 and began developing the first generation of Keurig coffee makers. These first models were designed for use in offices and commercial settings, where they quickly gained popularity due to their ease of use, convenience, and flavorful fresh coffee. In the following years, Keurig continued to develop and refine its coffee-making technology, releasing new models and expanding into the consumer market. The company also developed a wide range of coffee pods, known as "K-cups," which contained pre-measured portions of coffee and could be quickly and easily inserted into the Keurig machine for brewing. Notwithstanding its popularity, the Keurig coffee maker has been criticized for its environmental impact. The single-use K-cups are made from a combination of plastic and aluminum, making them neither easy to recycle nor quick to biodegrade. This has led to concerns about the millions of K-cups finding their way into landfills yearly.

In 2015, Sylvan expressed regret for having created the device. He acknowledged that he had not anticipated the scale of the waste problem and expressed remorse for his role in creating a product that contributes to environmental harm. Since then, Keurig has taken steps to address the environmental impact of its products, including the development of recyclable K-cups and encouraging customers to use refillable K-cup pods. The company has also launched a sustainability program to reduce waste and promote environmental stewardship. Despite these efforts, the Keurig coffee maker remains controversial, with critics arguing that the machine's convenience and ease of use still come at a steep environmental cost.

This case underlines our point that innovations should consider environmental impact at the outset. From a pricing perspective, the recommendation would be to increase the price of the pods or encourage the use of reusable coffee pods. One-use products such as plastic bottles and K-cups need to be priced higher in order to curtail their use. We have got things in the wrong order if products that are good for us and the planet are priced higher, whereas damaging ones are priced lower.

Key takeaways

Pricing is a critical factor influencing an innovation's market share, growth, and consumption patterns. When launching a new product or service, companies must consider pricing strategies in the context of their overall business strategy, competitive positioning, long-term growth goals, and societal and environmental impact.

- In the initial stages of product development, using pricing models that link pro-social behavior (discussed in Chapter 6) and strategies such as the "green premium" can help recover investment in R&D, differentiate products from conventional lines, and allow firms to experiment with new technology and establish the performance perception of the product. A long-term view of developing cost efficiencies and innovative monetization models in the initial stages is essential for long-term product and service viability.
- Pricing is also a critical factor in the later stages of the "diffusion of innovation." Companies can design pricing strategies that maximize adoption and profitability by understanding the needs and preferences of different user groups at each step of the diffusion process.
- As a whole, diffusion of innovation is a complex process and one that can have significant impacts on individuals, organizations, and society at large. Pricing strategies should be considered strategically at each stage to accelerate the adoption of products and services that improve the planet and society and decelerate the adoption of those that are not through managing increases or decreases in price, e.g., LED bulbs and plastic bottles.

Notes

1 Everett M. Rogers, *Diffusion of Innovations* (The Free Press, 1962).
2 Tom Huddleston Jr., "Remember These Failed Apple Products? They Were Some of the Tech Giant's Biggest Flops." CNBC Make It, September 1, 2018 (updated January 10, 2022). https://www.cnbc.com/2018/08/31/from-the-newton-to-lisa-failed-apple-products.html
3 Jim Amos, "MoviePass Shuts down for Good: The Meteoric Rise and Spectacular Fall of a Movie Industry Disruptor." *Forbes*, September 13, 2019. https://www.forbes.com/sites/jamos/2019/09/13/moviepass-shuts-down-for-good-the-meteoric-rise-and-spectacular-fall-of-a-movie-industry-disruptor/?sh=505924965c4c

4 Adrian Gore, Peter Harmer, Marc W. Pfitzer, and Nina Jais, "Can Insurance Companies Incentivize Their Customers to Be Healthier?," *Harvard Business Review*, June 23, 2017. https://hbr.org/2017/06/can-insurance-companies-incentivize-their-customers-to-be-healthier

Thomas Kolster, "Review of Discovery: Insurance That Bridges the Gap between Intent and Action." HSTalks, January 31, 2021. https://hstalks.com/t/4508/discovery-insurance-that-bridges-the-gap-between-i

5 Randi Kronthal-Sacco and Tensie Whelan, "Sustainable Market Share Index™". NYU Stern, March 2021. https://www.stern.nyu.edu/sites/default/files/assets/documents/Final%202021%20CSB%20Practice%20Forum-%207.14.21.pdf

6 E. Freya Williams, *Green Giants: How Smart Companies Turn Sustainability into Billion-Dollar Businesses* (Amacom, 2015): 154. https://openlibrary.org/books/OL26826759M/Green_Giants

7 Sherry Frey, Jordan Bar Am, Vinit Doshi, Anandi Malik, and Steve Noble, "Consumers Care about Sustainability – and Back It up with Their Wallets." McKinsey & Company, February 6, 2023. https://www.mckinsey.com/industries/consumer-packaged-goods/our-insights/consumers-care-about-sustainability-and-back-it-up-with-their-wallets

8 Camila Domonoske, "Tesla Slashes Prices across All Its Models in a Bid to Boost Sales." NPR Business, January 13, 2023. https://www.npr.org/2023/01/13/1149002185/tesla-prices-model-y-model-3-electric-cars-elon-musk

9 Leslie Patton, "McDonald's Pushing Meat as Salads Fail to Lure Diners." Bloomberg, May 29, 2013. https://www.bloomberg.com/news/articles/2013-05-29/mcdonald-s-pushing-meat-as-salads-fail-to-lure-diners#xj4y7vzkg

10 Cree, "Cree 100W Replacement LED review: Cree's bigger, brighter LED holds up to strong competition."2013. https://www.cnet.com/reviews/cree-100-watt-replacement-led-bulb-review/

11 "LED Lighting Market Size, Share, and COVID-19 Market Analysis." Fortune Business Insights. 2021. https://www.fortunebusinessinsights.com/led-lighting-market-106832

12 Zeineb Bouhlel, Jimmy Köpke, Mariam Mina, and Vladimir Smakhtin, *Global Bottled Water Industry: A Review of Impacts and Trends* (United Nations University Institute for Water, Environment and Health, 2023). https://inweh.unu.edu/wp-content/uploads/2023/03/UNU_BottledWater_Report_F.pdf

13 Alexandre Tanzi, "These Are the World's Most Expensive Places to Buy Water." Bloomberg, March 18, 2021. https://www.bloomberg.com/news/articles/2021-03-18/world-water-prices-diverge-massively-oslo-tel-aviv-costliest

14 "The Water Price Index (EUR)." *Holidu Magazine*. https://www.holidu.com/magazine/water-price-index-intl

15 "Why the Man behind Keurig's Coffee Pods Wishes He'd Never Invented Them." *The Guardian*, March 4, 2015.

4 Behavioral pricing for a better world faster

All that we are is the result of what we have thought.

Buddha

Price is one of the key determinants of consumer purchase decisions. How buyers process, remember and respond to price information is an integral part of marketing research. Behavioral pricing is a science of pricing that takes into account how buyers record, and uses price information to make purchase decisions. Behavioral pricing is founded on the idea that price can be considered a tangible stimulus, just like sound and light.[1] Extensive research has confirmed that price is not viewed objectively: the same price can be perceived differently by different people based on each individual's unique individual characteristics.

Between 1970 and 2000, there was a major upsurge in pricing and consumer research, which led to a deeper understanding of how consumers process price information. During this period, renowned scholars like Kent Monroe contributed seminal papers to the field.[2] The research used sophisticated experimental methods to investigate buyers' conscious and subconscious tendencies and explore objective and subjective contextual signals that influenced purchasing decisions. The role of price in marketing was further enhanced by examining the influence of price on brand name and quality perceptions. The notion was introduced that price is not just an economic variable but also a product attribute.[3] Additionally, price became widely recognized as an intrinsic cue for quality, alongside brand name and packaging.[4]

Research in the last couple of decades has focused on understanding how consumers perceive price and how they form decisions and evaluate products. More recently, research has been conducted on information acquisition, cognitive processing, remembering vs. knowing, and the attributes of price, quality, brand image, and fairness. Price fairness has an influence on customer satisfaction; and there is literature dealing with perceptions across the price–quality–brand nexus.[5] In the U.S., with a large percentage of sales now occurring online, there is a growing need to understand

DOI: 10.4324/9781032659008-5

the consumer psychology of online purchases. Online buyers exhibit different tendencies than in-store buyers: there is a higher level of price transparency in this environment and higher expectations of receiving the lowest price.[6] Both trust and uncertainty are higher online, with brand name and price often being taken as synonyms for quality. Research is ongoing to explore dynamic pricing strategies, personalized pricing, and pricing in social media. Companies already exploring personalized pricing include LexisNexis and Amazon.[7]

Marketers use this information to price products in a way that will work in the company's favor, i.e., customers will buy more of the product, buy higher-priced products, or buy more frequently. All these outcomes result in more sales and higher profits. However, the same tactics can be used to encourage the purchase of purpose-driven products. To understand how we can apply these principles, we will start with a quick review of the foundations of behavioral pricing.

The foundations of behavioral pricing

The "just-noticeable difference" theory

Ernst Weber, a 19th-century German anatomist and physiologist, pioneered the scientific quantification of human response to stimuli and is regarded as a founding father of experimental psychology. Weber observed that a subject could discern a difference in stimulus only if the weight difference between two objects exceeded a certain amount. Thus, if the weight difference was minor, the subject did not perceive it. This minimum threshold is known as the just-noticeable difference (JND).

Weber's student, Gustav Fechner, built on Weber's research and conducted his own experiments to quantify the relationship between stimuli and perception. He discovered a link between physical stimuli and their mental effects, which he termed "outer psychophysics." He also explored "inner psychophysics," proposing that physical stimuli contribute to human nervous system oscillations. The Weber–Fechner experiments formed the basis of the JND theory, which is still a foundational theory in psychology and is used in other fields that work with the human senses.

JND theory has also been extensively utilized in marketing to gain insights into perceptions of packaging, branding, pricing, and product size. Companies manage consumer perception by making changes to product size, color, labeling, and price based on JND thresholds. Negative changes are set below the threshold, while positive changes are set just above it. This theory is also useful in calibrating consumer perceptions of quality and price in order to improve profitability. For instance, when differences are not noticeable, manufacturers may substitute expensive materials for cheaper or more widely available ones or shrink the size of the product.

The JND theory has been used to gauge the effectiveness of sensory marketing, which makes use of all five human senses in creating perceptions of brands or brand personalities. The *Journal of Consumer Psychology* recently published a special issue on sensory perception and embodiment, describing how sensory inputs drive consumer behavior.[8] Companies have conducted experiments in improving sensory perception via smell in various contexts, including banking centers, cars, and pencils.

Kent Monroe's seminal work in the 1970s on behavioral pricing and JND, published in the *Journal of Marketing Research*, revolutionized the understanding of pricing. Pricing was no longer just a number; it was a number that could induce behavioral changes in consumers. His research revealed thresholds above or below which consumers will not alter their purchase intention.

Key concepts in behavioral pricing

1. **Internal reference price.** Behavioral price research is based on the notion that people evaluate prices comparatively, meaning they rely on an internal reference price as a basis for their judgments. An internal reference price is a dynamic and internal price against which individuals can compare the price of a product or service on offer.[9] It is subjective and varies depending on the individual and context. It could be a previous purchase price or a marketing message, an expected price, a sense of what is fair, or a general idea of the product's value. Also called a price stimulus, it's a mental representation that may not necessarily align with any actual real price. It is unique to each person, product category, sales environment, and moment in time. Other prices or numerical stimuli present during a price comparison process can also influence an individual's reference price.

2. The **differential perceptual threshold** is the level at which a buyer perceives that a price differs from their past experience or their expectation. The differential perceptual threshold is the smallest difference between two prices that can make an individual aware that the prices are distinct from one another. In other words, once this threshold has been reached, a buyer will have a perception of either expensiveness or cheapness. This doesn't necessarily mean that the buyer will change purchase behavior at this point. Also, even if the price objectively changes, the individual may not perceive that it has changed if the perceptual threshold

has not been reached. For example, if the price of your spaghetti sauce changed from $3.69 to $3.79, but you did not perceive that it was different, then the differential threshold has not been crossed. However, the threshold may well be crossed if the price goes from $3.69 to $3.99, and this time you perceive it as more expensive. You may still buy the sauce at $3.99, but it is with internal cognition that the price has increased or its become more expensive. Similarly, if the price goes down and you perceive it to be cheaper, it would be a differential perceptual threshold. Your behavior in both cases does not change, and you do not buy more or less of the item. You just note it to be more expensive or cheaper.

3. The **differential response threshold** is the point at which an individual responds to the pricing stimulus by changing behavior. At the lower end, if buyers perceive the price as a "deal," they may buy more and stockpile for the future. At the higher end, if buyers perceive the price as more expensive, they may reduce the quantity they purchase. So, whether or not people change their purchase behavior is a function of the *differential response threshold*. As a person's reference price level increases, larger actual price differences (increases or decreases) will be necessary to induce changes in *perceived* price differences. Estimates of the latitude of acceptable prices across various situations have ranged from ±2% to ±15% (or more) of the reference price.

4. An **absolute price threshold** is the point at which a buyer modifies their purchasing behavior in response to a perceived difference in price. The *low* absolute price threshold is the point below which a person may not buy the product because they doubt its quality or they are encouraged to buy more. The *high* absolute price threshold is the point beyond which a person loses their willingness to pay. Prices between the two thresholds are referred to as *acceptable price ranges* or latitudes of acceptable prices.

There is an exhaustive literature on behavioral pricing. What we've done here is outline some key concepts to be considered when pricing for societal benefit. Next, we apply these concepts in the context of incentivizing purpose-driven behaviors.

Leveraging behavioral insights to accelerate adoption

The price gap

The NYU Stern Center's 2022 sustainability report revealed that the price premium gap between eco-friendly and conventional products is approximately 29%.[10] *Bringing this gap down to more like 15% will make the adoption of these products faster.* This can be done in either of two ways: first, increase the price of current products or decrease the price of sustainable products. Second, leverage some of the strategies below to both minimize the retail price of sustainable products and, at the same time, increase the quality perception to justify the price premium.

When less is more

A strategy often used in retail is reducing the size of the product but keeping the price constant; this is known as "shrinkflation." Negative changes – such as product size or price increase – are generally set based on thresholds that consumers are less likely to notice; conversely, more positive changes – such as bigger size or promotional discounts – are set just above the noticeable threshold. Where price is concerned, increases or decreases of the same magnitude may not, in fact, be perceived equally.[11] Routinely, the package size is reduced just under the JND threshold with the price kept the same. During periods of inflation, companies often use this trick to avoid price increase perceptions. For example, in 2007, Birds Eye reduced the package size of its frozen peas from 907 g to 800 g with zero price change. Similarly, Palmolive reduced the size of its natural soap bar by 20% from 125 g to 100 g. So, essentially, someone who previously bought 10 soap bars a year will now need 12, resulting in a 20% increase in sales for Palmolive (see Table 4.1).

Table 4.1 Reductions in package size across eight branded items

Product	Current price	Previous size (g)	Current size (g)	Decrease (%)
Mars Bar	37p	62.5	58	7.20
Snickers	41p	62.5	58	7.20
Cadbury's Family Share chocolate bar	£1.38	250	230	8
Kraft Dairylea triangles (box of 8)	92p	180	160	11.10
Birds Eye frozen peas (reduced in 2007)	£1.69	907	800	11.80
Palmolive Naturals soap (reduced in 2006)	£1.00	125	100	20
Walkers crisps (multi-pack- reduced in 1998)	£1.25	27	25	7.40
Yorkie bar (reduced in 1995)	34p	65	52	20

Source: Adapted from Lost in Supermarkets, Nov. 2, 2012

To drive demand for eco-friendly goods, companies can price them within the acceptable range but reduce the size in order to manage the costs. This helps with the perception and increases the propensity to purchase.

In addition, from a behavioral point of view, the small package size may, in fact, promote a more conscious use of the product. If you have just a small amount of ketchup left, you will use less of it. Companies have traditionally promoted larger package sizes to encourage sales, but smaller package sizes may encourage more conscious consumption and make the product affordable.

The say–do gap

Customers claim they will pay more for eco-friendly products; but in reality, we are confronted by what is known as a "say–do gap." Although most consumers say they care about social and environmental issues, sustainability may not always translate to purchases because of a lack of willingness to pay higher prices, performance concerns, or skepticism about the benefits of environmentally friendly to broader society. The extent to which sustainability is a factor in consumer purchasing depends on the type of benefits consumers value for a specific product category. Many eco-friendly products suffer from *performance perception*, which is a major barrier to adoption. Many consumers are skeptical about sustainable products' capacity to yield the same quality or performance as their non-sustainable counterparts and do not completely buy into their negative impact on the planet. An article in the *Journal of Marketing*[12] showed that consumers associate higher ethicality with gentle attributes and lower ethicality with more solid attributes. As a result, the positive effect of sustainability considerations on consumer preferences actually diminishes when key functional attributes are highly valued, and this sometimes even results in preferences for less sustainable alternatives. This is known as the "sustainability liability." *Because of this, many firms downplay environmental benefits, especially in products where functional benefits are essential attributes.* These include diapers, laundry care, trash bags, etc., where consumers expect high performance; here, the eco alternatives have a lower market share. On the other hand, in those cases where "gentle" attributes are valued – yogurt, skin care, facial tissue, etc. – sustainability considerations positively impact consumer preferences. The article suggests that this "sustainability liability" can be minimized by providing explicit cues about product strength. This insight can help guide adjustments to the product offering, packaging, and marketing communications. Companies have largely tried to address this issue through tactical communication. You can see this on packaging in stores, with mes-saging designed to combat negative perceptions, or in advertising, where products are shown side by side to compare their effective-ness. The NYU Stern Center report (mentioned above) reviewed a range of products using Nielsen data. *The eco price premium was found to be similar across the majority of cases* – even for those products with high market share and adoption rates, but the adop-tion of environment products with "gentle" attributes was higher.[13] However, performance and impact skeptics remain plentiful and must be accounted for when introducing new products or changing existing ones.

We will now look at some research into the price–quality rela-tionship to see if we can find ways of combating the "say–do gap."

Managing performance perceptions effectively

Price and quality perceptions are intricately linked. Early research reviews suggest a positive correlation between price and perceived quality. So long as consumers are aware of a positive price–qual-ity relationship in a particular product market, they will use price as a signal of quality. However, conversely, if the price–quality relationship is weak, they will likely rely on intrinsic product information, such as product attributes, rather than extrinsic information, like price, to assess quality. Also, as consumers become more familiar with a product, they tend to rely on intrin-sic information. Consumers' use of price (or other extrinsic infor-mation) as a quality indicator depends on whether they perceive differences between various types of information across different product alternatives and whether they know about the actual price–quality relationships.

Communication of product attributes and building a strong per-formance perception of a product is therefore as important as pric-ing. *Informed consumers are less likely to rely on price information and more likely to consider intrinsic attributes when evaluating product quality.*[14] Electric car companies Tesla and Rivian have both positioned themselves as providers of high-performance vehi-cles that are better for the environment. They make no attempt to conceal the fact that their cars are electric; rather, they focus on performance and superior interiors in order to compete with tradi-tional luxury vehicles. The environmental attributes will drive pref-erence, but the message is that it does not mean compromising safety, speed, or style. When the Tesla car launched, the marketing campaigns emphasized performance, showing it pulling an airplane and driving on race tracks the tagline, "'better for the environment,' just came along for the ride." The price was also high, comparable to a high-end luxury car, which was a clear signal of high quality. Tesla went directly to market because it did not have confidence in the dealer network to effectively sell the car with this combination of attributes. Also, the opening hours and locations of franchises are more dealer-friendly than customer-friendly, whereas Tesla's showrooms are located in bustling metro areas and malls.

Creating the right links, signals, and cues is important in framing the performance image and accelerating the adoption of purpose-driven products. For example, consumers tend to associate specific categories of high-quality products with a certain country: watches from Switzerland or electronics from Japan are often perceived to be of higher quality than similar products from other countries. When it comes to sustainability, Sweden and Denmark are often noted as the countries with the highest standards. Wheat products from Europe are normally considered healthier because of their exclusion of GMO varieties.

Case: Cleaning products

Plant-based cleaning products are an eco-friendly alternative to traditional cleaning products, which tend to contain chemicals that can be harmful to human health and the environment. The Smithers study, The Future of Sustainable Cleaning Products to 2026 shows that in 2021, the total retail value of environmentally friendly laundry, surface care, dishwashing, and bath and shower goods was set to reach $72.9 billion. A forecast Compound Annual Growth Rate (CAGR) of 8.5% will drive the market to $109.7 billion in 2026. This contrasts with an overall market growth for all cleaning products of 4.1%, from $169.9 billion to $207.3 billion across 2021–2026. Cleaning products may, therefore, be suffering from a performance perception issue, i.e. sustainability liability. Emphasizing and communicating superior performance as a key differentiator is critical, whereas lowering the price may, in fact, hurt performance perception in the initial stages of the product lifecycle.

It is worth noting that there are exceptions where eco-products attain a strong performance perception from the outset. This can happen when large brand players in functional categories introduce their own eco-products.[15] For example, when Tide introduced its "Tide Clean" offering, this was against a background in which the brand in itself carried a reputation for reliability and strong performance. These attributes are then automatically transposed onto the eco-product in the minds of the consumers, i.e., "Tide sells good, strong products, so they are not likely to have introduced a new version if the quality was not good."

Research shows us that a *brand name* is the most influential extrinsic cue in determining perceived quality. The impact of brand names on quality perception is strengthened when combined with price information. Similarly, the influence of price on quality perception is amplified in the presence of a recognizable brand. Multiple mutually reinforcing signals are perceived as consistent indicators of quality.[16]

Warranties

To mitigate consumers' potential uncertainty about a product's quality, firms may use warranties. A guarantee that protects buyers against product failure is a signal of quality, with warranties for high-quality products typically more extensive and longer-lasting than those for low-quality products. This is because the cost of honoring warranties for low-quality products that fail (which they do more frequently) would be prohibitively high if the coverage was as comprehensive as their high-quality counterparts. Customers can, therefore, be confident that sellers offering extended coverage must be providing high-quality products.

Consumers are also more likely to perceive a warranty as a signal of quality if the seller is known for offering high-quality products. This is particularly true for buyers with low expertise in evaluating the merits of a warranty. In contrast, knowledgeable buyers are more likely to assess the warranty's merits rather than relying solely on the seller's reputation when they are evaluating product quality.

Warranties are, therefore, a useful tool in combating the low-performance perceptions that many environmentally-friendly products suffer from: they can assuage a consumer's uncertainty and incentivize purchase.

Anchoring

Anchoring is another means of influencing consumer perception of prices. Anchoring refers to the practice of setting an initial price, which serves as a reference point for subsequent prices. For example, if a company initially prices a product high but later reduces the price, consumers may perceive the discount as a gain and be more willing to purchase the product. The higher initial price creates a perception of high quality.

TJ Maxx is a popular American retailer known for offering discounted prices on a wide range of merchandise, including clothing, accessories, and home goods. In this chapter, we are elaborating on the pricing strategy it deploys. It employs an off-price retailing strategy, sourcing from its various suppliers discounted brand names and designer merchandise, such as overstocked items and irregulars, and items from closeouts. Its ever-changing inventory, with its well-known labels, is offered at deep discounts, creating a "treasure hunt" shopping experience. The store tag displays two prices: the selling price and the "Compare At" price. The "Compare At" price is the higher one: this *anchors* the consumers, thus communicating the deal the consumer is getting compared to the much lower selling price. In reality, the "Compare At" price is arbitrarily determined and does not necessarily represent the price it would have sold for at another department store. However it can be a useful tactic.

Price framing for online purchases

For products sold online, quality inferences are harder for the customer to make when the brand is not recognized. Moreover, perceived quality and perceived sacrifice (i.e., the sacrifice of paying more) may be affected when prices are partitioned into multiple components (e.g., item price and shipping charges). This difference in determining perceived quality may be due to the difficulty in assessing product quality online before purchase, which leads to a greater reliance on price as an indicator of quality. However, this increased perceived sacrifice may lead to greater price consciousness, particularly for price-sensitive consumers. In such cases, setting a slightly higher price – but below the price response threshold (<15% of reference price) – will signal higher quality to the online buyer but will lower the financial sacrifice.

Tell the price sooner rather than later

Pre-announcing the higher price of a higher-quality product in a long lead time helps a buyer adjust to the price. For example, in June 2023, Apple announced its Apple Vision Pro, a spatial computing headset, which it was going to sell at $3,499. Six months later, it unveiled its remarkable VR device, resembling a futuristic ski goggle. But why did Apple reveal the price a whole six months in advance? And why did it specify it as $3,499 and not a more general "around $3,500"?

Apple's strategy is a classic example of "behavioral pricing." It is an example of how timing affects our perception of prices. When we have a long time to wait before we can make a purchase, our attention tends to shift more toward the product's exciting features rather than its price. Conversely, if we receive the price information close to the moment of buying, that will be a more significant factor in the decision; it would feel more like a significant financial commitment.

This interesting phenomenon is referred to as "Psychological Distance." When you learn about a high-priced product with a release date far in the future, you're more likely to associate it with top-notch quality and eagerly anticipate its arrival. However, if that same product were only a few days away from being available, you might focus more on the effect it will have on your bank balance and hesitate to make the purchase. Announcing the price point and having time to plan for it makes it feel like less of a sacrifice. Have you ever had a dishwasher break on you? Most likely, you were price-sensitive when you were forced to buy a new one. Conversely, if you know a few months in advance that you will be buying a new dishwasher, you will likely buy a higher-priced one.

Psychological Distance plays a crucial role in determining how individuals prioritize different aspects of price. The opposite pattern emerges when it comes to perceived financial sacrifice in the short term. This suggests that when individuals use price as an indicator of product quality from a distant perspective, their judgment about that quality persists into later evaluations, leading to a decreased focus on sacrifice during near-time evaluations.[17] A consumer may think, "I don't want to pay more and still be unsure of the quality." *Because a higher price is viewed as a sacrifice, the unreliability of the product's quality may pose an additional barrier to purchase.*

The key takeaway here is simple: when a price might initially shock customers, it's beneficial to disclose it early on. By doing so, the initial shock dissipates, and customers can spend the intervening time getting excited about the fantastic product that awaits them. This strategy applies to any business that aims to create positive customer experiences and build anticipation for its offerings.

An understanding of the psychological aspects of pricing is a powerful tool for businesses. So, whether you're planning to launch a new sustainable product or a new monetization strategy, consider the impact of timing on customer perception: it can make a significant difference to their overall experience. When we have a long wait before making a purchase, we tend to focus more on the cool features and less on the price. However, if we're hit with the price information closer to the moment of purchase, the price suddenly becomes a bigger deal, and the purchase feels like a bigger sacrifice.

Key takeaways

This chapter discusses the role of behavioral pricing in incentivizing behaviors and how psychological techniques can be used to send signals and cues to change customer behavior.

- We discussed the issue of the price gap: how prices need to be within 15% and 17% of the reference price to encourage conversion to a product and greater than 15–17% to limit product adoption.
- Using strategies to reduce size when lower product consumption is desirable for social benefit using "just noticeable difference theory" is a way to manage usage and costs and keep prices stable.
- Primary research often overstates the market demand due to social bias; buyers say they will pay more, but often it does not translate to purchases in the store. Managers should be aware of this say–do behavior gap for environmentally marketed products.
- Similarly, managers cannot ignore the price–performance relationship when offering eco-friendly products. Encouraging trials and providing warranties are two ways of increasing consumer confidence in a product or service. For products where functional performance is key, successful strategies involve competing on key functional performance attributes as a differentiator rather than appealing to buyers' environmental consciousness.
- Price framing and communication are vital considerations relevant to in-store and online retailing. Behavioral tactics such as psychological distance in communicating price can be used to improve the adoption of a higher-priced product, particularly for new products.

Notes

1 K.B. Monroe, *Pricing: Making Profitable Decisions* (3rd edn; McGraw-Hill, 2003).
2 E.g., K.B. Monroe, "Buying Intentions and Purchase Probability: A Latent Structure Model Analysis." *Journal of Marketing Research* 8(3) (1971): 380–388.
3 A.R. Rao and D.A. Gautschi, "The Effect of Price, Brand Name, and Store Name on Buyers' Perceptions of Product Quality: An Integrative Review." *Journal of Marketing Research* 19(3) (1982): 345–357.
    Jagdish N. Bhagwati and T.N. Srinivasan, "Trade Policy and Development: What Have We Learned?" *American Economic Review* 72(2) (1982): 231–246.
4 Valarie A. Zeithaml, "Consumer Perceptions of Price, Quality, and Value: A Means–End Model and Synthesis of Evidence." *Journal of Marketing* 52(3) (1988): 2–22.
5 Exploring this idea at a global level in J.N. Sheth and A. Parvatiyar, "Relationship Marketing in Consumer Markets: Antecedents and Consequences." *Journal of the Academy of Marketing Science* 23(4) (2001): 255–271.
6 S. Ba and P.A. Pavlou, "Evidence of the Effect of Trust Building Technology in Electronic Markets: Price Premiums and Buyer Behavior." *MIS Quarterly* 26(3) (2002): 243–268.

7 P. Chatterjee and J.M. McGinnis, "A Portfolio Analysis of Brand Positioning Strategies." *Journal of Marketing Research* 47(4) (2010): 594–607.

D. Grewal, K.L. Ailawadi, D. Gauri, K. Hall, P. Kopalle, S.A. Neslin, … and B.A. Weitz, "Innovations in Retail Pricing and Promotions." *Journal of Retailing* 87(S1) (2011): S43–S52.

F.L. Weisstein, K.B. Monroe, and M. Kukar-Kinney, "Retail Price Advertising: Joint Effects of Multiple Cues." *Journal of Retailing* 89(2) (2013): 149–165. https://link.springer.com/article/10.1007/s13162-013-0041-1

8 Aradhna Krishna and Norbert Schwarz, "Sensory Marketing, Embodiment, and Grounded Cognition: A Review and Introduction." *Journal of Consumer Psychology* 24(2) (2014): 159–168. https://doi.org/10.1016/j.jcps.2013.12.006

9 Weisstein, Monroe, and Kukar-Kinney, *op. cit.*

10 Randi Kronthal-Sacco and Tensie Whelan, "Sustainable Market Share Index: 2021 Report." NYU Stern Center for Sustainable Business, April 2022.

11 Kent B. Monroe, "Buyers' Subjective Perceptions of Price." *Journal of Marketing Research* 10(1) (1973): 70–80. https://doi.org/10.1177/002224377301000110

12 M.G. Luchs, R.W. Naylor, J.R. Irwin, and R. Raghunathan, "The Sustainability Liability: Potential Negative Effects of Ethicality on Product Preference." *Journal of Marketing* 74(5) (2010): 18–31. https://doi.org/10.1509/jmkg.74.5.018

13 Kronthal-Sacco and Whelan, *op. cit.*

14 A.R. Rao and K.B. Monroe, "The Moderating Effect of Prior Knowledge on Cue Utilization in Product Evaluations." *Journal of Consumer Research* 15(2) (1988): 253–264.

R.N. Yan and J. Sengupta, "Effect of Price-Related Advertising Cues on Consumer Perceptions of Quality: A Reference Price Perspective." *Journal of Marketing* 75(3) (2011): 48–59.

15 Kronthal-Sacco and Whelan, *op. cit.*

16 A.R. Rao and K.B. Monroe, "The Effect of Price, Brand Name, and Store Name on Buyers' Perceptions of Product Quality: An Integrative Review." *Journal of Marketing Research* 26(3) (1989): 351–357.

J.B. Smith and P. Natesan, "Remembrance of Things Past: The Meaning of Recall and Recognition for Brand Name Recognition." *Journal of Consumer Research* 25(4) (1999): 340–350.

A.D. Miyazaki, D. Grewal, and R.C. Goodstein, "The Effect of Multiple Extrinsic Cues on Quality Perceptions: A Matter of Consistency." *Journal of Consumer Research* 32(2) (2005): 146–153.

17 Torsten Bornemann and Christian Homburg, "Psychological Distance and the Dual Role of Price." *Journal of Consumer Research* 38(3) (October 1, 2011): 490–504. https://doi.org/10.1086/659874

Part II

Bringing stakeholders along

5 The role of government policy

Taxes are the price we pay for a civilized society.
Oliver Wendell Holmes Jr.

Government intervention in pricing typically appears in one of two forms: disincentive (a tax or tariff) or an incentive (subsidy or tax credit). Taxes can act to penalize firms and individuals that resist the necessary changes toward more socially benevolent practices. Tariffs can similarly work as disincentives. Subsidies, on the other hand, work like price discounts to provide incentives and encourage certain types of behaviors.

Typically, subsidies and tax credits are loans or payouts the government gives (to both individuals and businesses) to encourage a particular activity. The World Trade Organization uses a broader definition of subsidies to include any financial benefit the government provides. This can include grants, tax concessions including exemptions, deferrals, loan guarantees, any policy paying more than the market price, or stock purchases that keep prices higher. *Subsidies and tax credits effectively act like price discounts.* See Figure 5.1 for a schematic of types of government intervention.

The U.S. government provides agricultural subsidies to assist farmers in navigating the challenges posed by fluctuations in production and profitability stemming from factors such as weather conditions and market dynamics. In 2021, these subsidies amounted to $28.5 billion, with the Department of Agriculture serving as the primary federal agency responsible for directly disbursing funds to farmers. In contrast, subsidies exclusive to the oil and gas sector impose an annual cost of approximately $4 billion on U.S. taxpayers. Nationwide housing subsidies in the U.S. cover less than 4% of the housing stock, a significant difference from Western Europe, where such subsidies range from 15 to 40%. Additionally, the U.S. government offers incentives such as the Investment Tax Credit to reduce federal taxes for homeowners adopting solar power systems. Furthermore, various U.S. states have been competing for

DOI: 10.4324/9781032659008-7

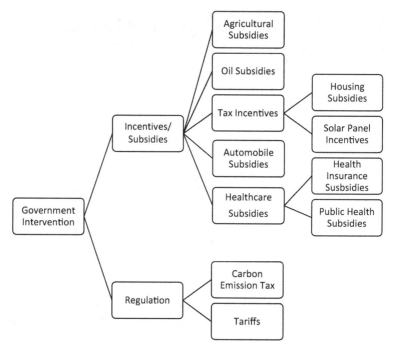

Figure 5.1 Types of government intervention.

new auto plants, with 17 states granting $17 billion in incentives to attract domestic and foreign automakers. The Affordable Care Act (ACA), also known as Obamacare, extends health insurance subsidies in the form of tax credits to make coverage more affordable for middle- and low-income individuals.

The U.S. Environmental Protection Agency (EPA) allocates over $4 billion in grants and various assistance agreements annually. The EPA collaborates with various entities, including small nonprofit organizations and large state governments, to support numerous visionary organizations pursuing environmental objectives.

The key issue that arises is: what is the role of government, via interventions, programs, and subsidies, in accelerating the change to greener technologies and improving quality of life? What strategies and policies are sustainable and successful in accelerating the adoption of pro-social products and services? How can the government, people, and corporations unite to make the sustainability transition? Will government support – sharing the cost borne by firms when moving to greener technologies – accelerate our journey to a sustainable planet? How do such considerations affect managers in their daily work? And how can grants support and offset costs for firms and hence prices to buyers?

A manager working on developing a pricing strategy for a sustainable product might wish to explore options for subsidies and financial incentives in their industry – possibly to reduce some of the upfront costs associated with the change to greener technologies, i.e., the use of solar energy or electric cars. In an effort to foster innovation and drive the development of transformative technologies like renewable energy, carbon capture, waste management, and energy efficiency, governments are providing subsidies and grant funding to research institutes, academic institutions, and private R&D firms. Managers are well advised to leverage these financial incentives and to lobby for better policies to support the industry.

We present some cases below as examples. This does not pretend to be a comprehensive list but it does provide a flavor of the role of government. The cases discuss government financial incentives and policies and their corresponding effects on the environment, healthcare, quality of life, food and water prices, and consumption.

Environment

Solar panels tax credit

One form of subsidy is a tax credit. For example, in 2006, the federal government approved an Investment Tax Credit (ITC) for solar panels, which lowered the price of a solar panel by 40% in 2023.[1] Governmental incentives and policies have a significant role to play in the take-up of solar panels. California is the king of solar panel adoption and the 2020 policy to have all new homes fitted with solar will undoubtedly increase the penetration of solar power. This move will cut fossil-fuel energy use in new homes by over 50% – the equivalent of taking 115,000 gasoline cars off the road.[2] However, other states, like Texas, offer no incentives for households to install solar panels. The economics are different there, as electricity is cheaper, and Texans would require a longer time horizon to recoup their investments. However, having incentives will help move things faster towards better energy solutions.

In Europe, Germany's feed-in tariff program guaranteed a fixed payment for every unit of electricity generated by solar panels, encouraging solar adoption. Although this program was planned to be phased out, it served as a significant incentive for years. Australia's Renewable Energy Target (RET) program mandates that a certain percentage of electricity in Australia should come from renewable sources, including solar. This led to the creation of renewable energy certificates (RECs) that could be traded or used to reduce the cost of solar installations. India's government launched various subsidy programs at the state and central levels to promote solar power adoption. These subsidies aimed to make solar energy more affordable for residential, commercial, and industrial consumers.

Price, once again, plays a crucial role in driving people one way or another. Different strategies – price reductions in the form of rebates or lobbying to increase the price of electricity – can work together in pushing customers toward better forms of energy. Forms of price incentives include tax incentives, rebates, and paying for solar electricity. Unfortunately, tax incentives usually work only for higher-income households, thus limiting the penetration of solar power. Rebates in the form of price reductions can be more effective. Other monetization models, such as third-party ownership, can also stimulate growth. Another key price-related factor that can influence solar panel adoption is the rate at which the local government purchases the power generated by the panels. *A much-reduced electric bill – or possibly even receiving revenue for power generated – can be a huge incentive for homeowners.* However, many local electric companies do not pay market rates for power generated by households – but that may be changing.

Electric vehicle tax credit

In 2021, approximately 66% of newly registered passenger vehicles in Norway were fully electric, underscoring the nation's remarkable progress in promoting electric vehicle adoption. This achievement can be largely attributed to a range of generous fiscal incentives, such as exemptions from registration taxes, from VAT, and from motor fuel taxes for zero-emission vehicles (ZEVs), along with significant reductions – of at least 50% – in road taxes, ferry fares, and parking fees for EV owners. These financial incentives have played a pivotal role in stimulating consumer demand for ZEVs and boosting their representation within the country's vehicle fleet. Given the undeniable success of its electric mobility policies, the government is now developing a sustainable vehicle taxation system to further support this transformative shift in transportation.

Another example is the U.S. government's subsidy for electric cars, which has made electric vehicles more prevalent and affordable. A less direct subsidy can be discerned in the way the promotion of electric vehicles is changing the automobile industry itself, although this could also be viewed as an environmental subsidy. In 2010, the U.S. federal government began offering tax credits upwards of $2,500 to purchase plug-in electric vehicles. The credit increases for higher kilowatts, maxing out at $7,500. This incentivization for consumers and businesses to purchase electric vehicles means manufacturers have a greater incentive to produce them.[3] However, at the same time, many states charge fees annually to EV car owners to compensate for the fuel tax. The fee ranges from $50 to $200 annually and is a disincentive to purchase an electric vehicle.

In Singapore, too, the government is encouraging the adoption of electric vehicles, offering rebates of up to S$45,000 for those choosing the electric route.[4] Another alternative is to put a disincentive on the purchase of new cars by making them cost-prohibitive and rationing the number of people that can buy a car (see box below).

Case: Vehicle taxes in Singapore

The Singapore government regulates the number of vehicles sold. Singapore is an expensive place to buy a car. The country – home to just 5.6 million people and traversable in under an hour – has a distinctive quota system that regulates the number of cars nation-wide. Vehicles are sold with a ten-year "certificate of entitlement" (COE), the cost of which is integrated into the vehicle's price. The limited availability of COEs, which are acquired through a competitive bidding process, makes Singapore's car prices the highest in the world. For instance, a standard Toyota Corolla Altis currently commands around S$141,000 (US$98,885) in Singapore, inclusive of registration fees and taxes, in stark contrast to the US$22,000 price tag in the United States. COE prices have surged dramatically in recent months due to heightened demand following the reopening post-Covid and an influx of affluent foreign nationals, notably from Hong Kong. In the most recent bi-monthly bidding, COEs now cost 40–50% more than they did in the same period the previous year across various major private car categories, and an astounding 120–170% more than in 2020.

Carbon pricing

The practice of calculating the carbon footprint of products, which quantifies their climate impact in terms of carbon dioxide equivalent (CO_2eq) emissions per unit, has become widespread. As we discussed in Chapter 2, carbon pricing involves putting a monetary value on carbon emissions to address climate change. It aims to capture the external costs of carbon pollution, such as damage to crops and health – and, not least, as a "greenhouse gas" leading to climate change – and ties them to their sources through a carbon price. This approach shifts responsibility back to polluters, who can then choose to reduce emissions or pay for them, known as carbon offsetting.

Governments and NGOs play an important role in regulating the price and quality of carbon. There are two main methods of carbon pricing: emissions trading systems (ETS) and carbon taxes. ETS sets a cap on emissions and allows low-emission industries to sell allowances to larger emitters, establishing a market price for emissions. Carbon taxes, on the other hand, directly set a price for carbon content. The choice of method depends on national circumstances. Over 40 countries and 20 cities, states, and provinces already use carbon pricing mechanisms, covering about half of their emissions, which amounts to approximately 13% of global greenhouse gas emissions. This fiscal approach is aimed at encouraging cleaner options and innovation while reducing emissions.

An article in the *Journal of Marketing*, which discusses the role of carbon footprint on product design and price,[5] notes that while carbon regulation effectively controls the overall climate impact of organizations, it may inadvertently lead to an increase in a product's carbon footprint. It may be cheaper for corporations to buy carbon credits rather than try to reduce their carbon emissions. On the other hand, carbon taxation can raise a product's costs without necessarily reducing the company's carbon footprint. Their research suggests that society should establish a set price for carbon emissions. Carbon offsets and carbon taxes supposedly serve this purpose. However, carbon offsets may not sufficiently incentivize firms to invest in greener technologies, making them more suitable as an interim measure until new eco-friendly technologies become available. Notably, the United Nations Global Compact has issued a call to set an internal price of at least $100 per metric ton, believing that pricing carbon emissions will prioritize climate change in corporate strategies.[6]

Many governments are pushing toward higher carbon taxation to disincentivize carbon output and accelerate the transition to green technologies. Firms designing new products should consider the impact of taxation on their overall costs. However, government regulation is typically behind the curve, so forward-looking companies that already include carbon costs in their calculations will have a competitive edge in the long run and be better equipped to succeed – provided they do it strategically. Already some regions, such as the European Union, India, and California, are pushing the envelope for responsible reporting.

Oil subsidies

The U.S. government used subsidies as long ago as World War I, in order to stimulate oil and gas production and ensure continuous domestic supply. A much more recent example of a subsidy in favor of the oil industry is the Deepwater Royalty Relief Act of 1995, in which Congress allowed oil companies to drill on federal properties royalty-free. Oil subsidies like these are now coming under scrutiny from policymakers and community members across the globe, as they represent the wrong price incentives from the point of view of our environment and planetary wellbeing. An article published by the Brookings Institution elaborates on the issues with subsidizing fossil fuels.[7] One of the primary charges against the artificial lowering of prices is that it leads to overconsumption, especially in capital- and energy-intensive companies such as transport and power. Companies lose the financial incentive to reduce use, which in turn has an impact on air pollution and health. The oil subsidies remain substantial, and there has been some discussion in the U.S. about withdrawing the $4 billion in oil subsidies and using it for other purposes instead. As reported by the Environmental and Energy Study Institute,[8] direct subsidies to the fossil fuel industry totaled $20 billion per year. Almost 80% of it goes towards oil and gas. Tax revenue lost because of these subsidies is estimated at around $11.5 billion, which theoretically could be used for societal benefit.

The reality is that if gasoline becomes expensive, consumers will find other solutions and use less of it: carpooling to work, making shorter vacation trips, etc. *A high gasoline price can be used as a lever to reduce consumption, hence lowering the supply pressure.*

In many European countries, excise taxes are considerably higher than in other parts of the world. These taxes can account for a significant portion of the retail price of fuel. For instance, in the U.K., France, and Germany, the tax component of gasoline price can account for 60% or even more of the total price per liter. By imposing such high taxes on oil and fuel, European governments effectively raise the cost of using fossil fuels for transportation, which serves as a disincentive for excessive consumption and encourages the adoption of more fuel-efficient vehicles, alternative energy sources, and the use of public transportation. This taxation strategy not only reduces carbon emissions but also generates revenue that can be invested in sustainable transportation infrastructure and initiatives.

Greenpeace is a global network of independent campaigning organizations working to expose global environmental problems and promote solutions for a green and peaceful future.[9] Price incentives, they say, should be offered in areas where the government seeks to encourage activity; oil and gas is not an industry that needs subsidies at this juncture, and funds would be better directed elsewhere, such as renewables. However, removing subsidies is not always so simple: it can have significant economic consequences. When the Philippines discontinued its oil subsidy, the price of gasoline shot up, which had a big impact on the Philippines, economy. Similarly, Indonesia removed its subsidies in 2005, and fuel prices subsequently went up by 30%.[10] Low-income families had to be supported through the transition. Jordan also gradually eased out of its subsidies in 2005, but by 2008, domestic fuel prices were falling into line with international prices. Behavioral pricing tells us that any benefit that has been given away for a long enough time becomes a buyer expectation or reference price. Therefore, a transition in which a benefit is removed must be done strategically and slowly, protecting the most vulnerable groups and minimizing economic impact.

Housing subsidies

Housing subsidies promote home ownership. They can come in the form of interest rate subsidies or down-payment assistance. The U.S. federal government incentivizes first-time homebuyers through its Federal House Administration (FHA) loans. Backed by the Department of Housing and Urban Development (HUD), these loans allow lenders to help borrowers who might not otherwise qualify for a mortgage.[11]

Housing subsidies, when designed and implemented with "purpose-driven" principles in mind, can contribute to sustainable and inclusive housing solutions. They can address social inequalities by making decent and affordable housing accessible to low-income individuals and marginalized communities, reducing homelessness, and enhancing the quality of life for disadvantaged populations. *Firms can leverage these subsidies to create affordable and green housing for their employees.* For example, housing subsidies can be structured to incentivize – or stipulate – environmentally friendly practices. They can be tied to energy-efficient house design, integration of renewable energy, or sustainable construction materials.

Subsidies can specifically target affordable housing initiatives, providing financial assistance to either developers or tenants. They can even be integrated into broader community development initiatives, focusing on revitalizing neighborhoods, enhancing infrastructure, and fostering social cohesion. By considering the social and economic needs of the communities in this way, housing subsidies can contribute to sustainable urban development and promote thriving, inclusive neighborhoods.

Healthcare

The government plays a major role in healthcare and its involvement can take a variety of different forms. It can offer subsidies for healthcare, mandate the behavior of pharmaceutical companies, launch public health initiatives (e.g., anti-smoking or pro-vaccination campaigns), and penalize firms that engage in activities that are harmful to public health. Below we discuss some government interventions that use pricing mechanisms.

Public health: Covid-19 vaccine pricing strategy

As the world confronted the Covid-19 pandemic in 2020, the U.S. was among many countries that started working on developing vaccines. Not only was the vaccine created quickly, it was given to everyone and at no cost. As business school professors, we are not fans of "free." However, in this case, providing the vaccine at no cost removed the key potential barrier to universal uptake and helped in effecting a penetration of 70%.[12] Now, 97% of the population has immunity from infection.

Not only did the government offer it for free to all citizens, including visitors and non-registered immigrants, but it also provided incentives to get the shot, such as free childcare and rides to vaccination sites. Some states offered rewards, ranging from entry into million-dollar lotteries and scholarships to free food and drinks. Private companies joined in, too, with incentive programs for their employees (paid time off, sweepstakes) and customers.

The Harvard Medical School conducted an analysis of these various incentives,[13] showing that incentive programs are effective and increase vaccine uptake but that the effectiveness varies based on the demographics of the state population. An earlier study program, in 1996, had a lottery-type incentive – a prize of $50 in grocery gift cards – to encourage patients from lower-income groups to be vaccinated for influenza. Vaccine uptake increased to 29%; a 9% increase. Similarly, in 1984, a lottery program was launched to promote childhood vaccinations, with three prize values, $100, $50, and $25, based on the number of overdue immunizations.[14] This incentive resulted in a higher vaccination rate of 22.5%, compared to 5.9% in the control group. Once again, in 1995, another study looked at vaccination incentives, this time targeting measles immunization in New York preschool children,[15] with the incentives varying from ride services to food vouchers. The result? Those sites that offered the incentives saw 2.9 times the uptake. The study found similar results when they targeted the primary care physician groups who are actually administering the vaccine. The incentive rewarded the groups who achieved a vaccination rate of above 70% with a 10% increase over their regular fees; physician groups who achieved a rate of 85% got a 20% bonus. The uptake in the incentivized groups was 73.1% compared to 55.7% in the control group.

There are examples of straightforward cash inducements, too, at the point of vaccination. In Sweden, cash payments for taking the Covid-19 vaccine increased uptake by 4.3%. In the U.S., North Carolina awarded $25 to those taking the vaccine and even awarded those who drove someone to the vaccination site. However, it has to be said that there are instances where incentives, lotteries especially, have not made a difference.

There are, of course, ethical considerations and concerns around coercion and manipulation. However, based on these studies, it is hard to deny that incentives work. *The studies tell us that monetary incentives are the most effective, and lottery-type incentives are least effective.*

Food prices and health

Researchers at Tufts University and Imperial College evaluated the relationship between food the prices and mortality. Their study concluded that lowering the prices of healthy foods, such as fruit and vegetables, by 30% can result in 63,000 fewer deaths every year. The second part of the study tested for providing healthy incentives to lower socio-economic strata. Program participants received 30% more per dollar but could only spend the extra on fruit and vegetables. Participants who received the incentive bought more fruits and vegetables than their control-group counterparts.[16] Conversely, an increase in the prices of items reduces consumption.

The recommendations from the study are not to replace crop and soybean subsidies with subsidies for broccoli and apples; rather, they encourage the government to reduce prices of healthy foods for the end-consumer – a more effective strategy. In the long run, effective pricing can reduce cardiovascular diseases and deaths by making healthy choices accessible and affordable. This, in turn, reduces social health costs over the long term.

In Singapore, the Health Promotion Board (HPB) responded to escalating rates of obesity and type 2 diabetes in the country. Starting in 2015, eateries in Singapore that offer healthier food options – such as being cooked in low-saturated-fat cooking oil – received an HPB subsidy under the Healthier Ingredient Subsidy scheme.[17] In the first phase, suppliers who introduce cooking oils containing less than 35% saturated fat will receive a subsidy of

50 cents per kilogram. This figure, determined collaboratively by industry experts, will be subject to biannual reviews. In Singapore, white rice and refined grain noodles constitute a substantial portion of the typical diet, so the initiative will expand over the next three years to include, among other things, whole-grain noodles, wholemeal bread, and brown rice. The aim is to bridge the price gap between healthier and conventional ingredients, ultimately fostering greater demand for healthier choices among consumers.

The HPB has also partnered with major supermarket chains to incentivize new habits,[18] offering discounts and promoting whole-grain rice while emphasizing through signage the health benefits of brown and red rice. These collaborations also involve distribution of educational materials and "nutrition toolkits" containing guides and recipes to facilitate consumers' transition to whole grains. These efforts have yielded positive results, with supermarket chain Cold Storage reporting a 15% increase in whole-grain rice sales and a 10% decrease in white rice sales over three years, while its competitor NTUC FairPrice achieved a remarkable 40% boost in brown-rice sales within six months of introducing discounts on whole-grain rice products.

Tobacco tax

The U.S. government's highly effective program to reduce tobacco consumption has had a multi-pronged approach, which includes increasing effective consumer prices. As it becomes cost-prohibitive for many, particularly younger adults, fewer people are exposed to the risks of acquiring the habit. A recent World Health Organization (WHO) article noted that several countries have reported positive outcomes by introducing taxes on cigarettes to raise the prices. Gambia, for example, substantially reduced cigarette use, increased its tax revenue, and decreased cigarette imports. Through regular increases in excise taxes on cigarettes, Sri Lanka achieved a particularly high taxation level, with close to 77% of the price of a pack being taxed. An ultimately threefold increase resulted in a 34% drop in cigarette consumption and an almost doubling of excise tax revenues earmarked for universal health coverage. In Oman, the proportion of tax on the price of the most popular brand of cigarettes increased from 25% to almost 64% between 2018 and 2020.[19]

The WHO also notes a decline in lung cancer rates, which have halved from the mid-1970s to 2009, a period in which cigarette prices doubled.[20] *The models confirm that pricing does impact long-term health outcomes.* The U.S. government has taken similar measures with regard to sugary beverages in order to combat obesity and diabetes.

Aside from levying taxes, there is an important role for government to play in setting price minimums, and limiting discounts, on harmful products.

Pharmaceutical drug pricing

Where there is a lack of regulation for pharmaceutical companies, cases of price hikes in life-saving drugs such as Daraprim (a brand name of pyrimethamine), insulin, and EpiPen (epinephrine auto-injectors) exemplify an interesting dilemma. The high prices are often framed as an alternative between investment in research and development (R&D) and the affordability of medications.

Many companies in the pharmaceutical industry charge a price premium for products, resulting in higher revenues and profit margins. One view is that higher profits coming from pharmaceutical innovation incentivize investment in R&D, leading to more innovation. This results in cures for diseases and illnesses, potentially benefitting society and people's quality of life. Higher profits in this schema is what drives pharmaceutical companies to find new solutions to health problems. Developing new drugs is expensive, and a significant return on investment creates the necessary incentive. This, in turn, benefits consumers by providing a wider range of drugs and medicines. Patent protection is the government mechanism to support firms' investment in innovation. Higher prices represent one way of ensuring companies are incentivized to innovate. But are there other ways?

In recent years, insulin prices have led to public outrage. And, in response to growing pressure, several pharmaceutical companies – Eli Lilly, Novo Nordisk, and Sanofi – have reduced their insulin prices. Insulin pricing has long been a contentious issue, and has led to legislative efforts such as the Affordable Insulin Act, which set a price cap of $35 for insulin copays for Medicare patients over the age of 65. However, there have been calls for wider action to address insulin costs for all citizens, and bipartisan bills have been introduced to cap insulin costs across the board. Between 2012 and 2019 the list price of insulin doubled. In 2014, manufacturers received $70 per every $100 spent on insulin, with Pharmaceutical Benefit Managers (PBMs) receiving $30. However, by 2018, manufacturers were only receiving $47, whereas PBMs were getting $53.[21]

The high insulin prices have been blamed on a dysfunctional rebate system involving the PBMs, consistent price gouging, and flaws in the healthcare system. Some diabetics have had to resort to risky behaviors like purchasing insulin from unauthorized online pharmacies. In a further move, in 2023 President Biden identified ten drugs the prices of which were to be renegotiated for Medicare/ Medicaid. Pharmaceutical pricing continues to be a point in political debates in the U.S. Global price in drug pricing is an opportunity for international arbitrage for many as the same drug is available at significantly lower prices in other parts of the world. In 2015, when Epipens became expensive, many people drove to Canada to purchase the medicine at a fraction of the price.

Food and water prices

Agricultural subsidies

There have been farm subsidies in the U.S. since the 1920s, put in place to help manage the supply and demand of agricultural goods. The government offers the farmers a price that is high enough for them to remain profitable but not so high that they produce more than the demand. By controlling the supply, i.e. agricultural production, the government can more easily manage the pricing. Also, farmers may choose not to maximize crop production but leave some land unused. By thus controlling crop production and managing supply, the government can get higher prices for crops in the global markets and simultaneously lower farmers' costs. Sometimes, the government will buy up agricultural overproduction in order to store it or disburse free to low-income countries. On average, agricultural subsidies over the last decade (2013–2022) have amounted to around $17.6 billion a year.[22] *For the most part, these agricultural subsidies have prevented food waste and made farming an economically viable activity in the United States.*

The U.S. government has historically exerted control over cheese and wheat production by offering subsidies and implementing a range of agricultural policies designed to support farmers and maintain a steady food supply. First are the Price Support Programs, where the government sets a minimum price, known as the "support price," for commodities such as wheat and dairy products, including cheese. If market prices dip below this threshold, the government purchases surplus goods at the support price, ensuring farmers receive a guaranteed income even when the market price is low.

Direct payments to farmers, based on factors such as the amount of cultivated land and historical production of specific crops, also serve as a form of income support. Some subsidies even incentivize the production of particular crops – like wheat and dairy – as part of broader agricultural strategies.

Marketing orders, used especially in the dairy sector, regulate production by establishing quotas for cheese and other dairy products. Farms that surpass these limits may face penalties, while those adhering to quotas may receive price premiums. These measures help manage cheese production, avoiding surpluses and price fluctuations. Export subsidies have been used, too, to enhance the competitiveness of American agricultural products, including cheese and wheat, in global markets. These can take the form of financial assistance to exporters or the sale of surplus commodities to foreign nations at reduced prices.

U.S. farm bills, periodically passed by Congress, lay out the framework for agricultural policies, influencing cheese and wheat production through subsidy programs. Moreover, certain environmental and conservation programs tie subsidies to responsible farming practices. Farmers adopting specific conservation measures may qualify for extra subsidies, which can influence their production choices.

Notably, agricultural policies and subsidy programs evolve over time in response to economic conditions, trade agreements, and political priorities. Their overarching objective is to maintain agricultural stability, safeguard farmer incomes, and guarantee a reliable food supply.

Water tariffs

The Organization for Economic Co-operation and Development (OECD), headquartered in Paris, France, is an international organization comprising 38 member countries dedicated to promoting democracy and fostering market economies. The organization claims that, where water is concerned, *price* is the key to encouraging people to waste less, pollute less, and invest more in water infrastructure. Pricing can indeed play an important part in encouraging pro-social behaviors, as we have seen. Water costs vary significantly across countries; most do not factor in the investment in sanitation and the filtration systems needed to produce clean water.[23] As we discussed in Chapter 2, in this example, the *social cost* of water will be much higher.

Quality of life

Governmental regulation to control prices can play a key role in using prices to leverage societal change. Most states in the U.S. have laws against price gouging. These laws are in place to limit the maximum price that can be charged for specified goods. California has set a 10% ceiling on price increases; other states set it at 25%. Price gouging is often rigorously prohibited in a declared period of emergency or disaster. This usually covers essential items such as food, water, housing, and gas.

Below is a quick rundown of U.S. governmental regulations related to pricing:

- **Sherman Anti-Trust Act (1890):** specifically addresses issues related to price fixing, exchanging price information, and price signaling.
- **Clayton Act (1914):** prohibits anticompetitive mergers, tying arrangements, exclusive dealing agreements, interlocking directorates, and the acquisition of stock in competitor companies.
- **Federal Trade Commission Act (1914):** prohibits "unfair methods of competition in commerce, and unfair or deceptive acts of practices in commerce."
- **Robinson–Patman Act (1936):** prohibits anticompetitive practices by producers, specifically price discrimination.

Other activities related to price which are discouraged by the state are:

- **Price fixing:** a pre-setting of prices of products by restricting output, agreeing to divide markets, or restricting the forces of competition.
- **Exchange price information:** collecting price information from members of an association and disseminating it to the members.
- **Parallel pricing:** companies act in a concerted way, working with a price leader, to achieve a common understanding to overprice.
- **Predatory pricing:** cutting prices to unreasonably low or unprofitable levels to drive competitors from the market.
- **Collusion:** a premise of antitrust law is that collusion among business rivals inevitably leads to a monopoly outcome, typically higher prices and profits shared by a group of organizations.

These are all areas in which the U.S. (and other) governments work to prevent companies from unfairly controlling prices, charging people exorbitant prices, or creating uncompetitive environments. In many state-organized programs, price changes have to go through a rigorous approval process. For example, Marta, Atlanta's public transit system, is limited to a certain number of price increases per year, the maximum levels of which are also imposed.

In countries like the U.S., where free-market economics has become the leading dynamic, it is easy to underestimate the crucial role that government regulation has to play in controlling and constraining that dynamic. In celebrating the innovative power of competitive market forces, we should remember that, left unchecked, they can exacerbate inequalities in society. Government interventions have long been a pro-social force for good, well before the notion took off in the business community in the last few decades. A centralized hand on the rudder of pricing can curb the worst excesses and preserve lower-income citizens from being further impoverished and excluded.

Case: Dynamically priced HOV lanes in Atlanta

Highway lanes in the I-85 corridor north of I-285 in Atlanta are dynamically priced based on traffic. The Corridor express lanes offer a range of toll rates based on demand and time of travel. During peak hours, the tolls range from $0.10 to $0.90 per mile, while off-peak hours have a flat rate of $0.50 per trip. As demand increases, the toll amounts rise to deter traffic and maintain reliable travel times for motorists using the express lanes. Toll rate signs display the current rate, allowing drivers to make an informed decision about whether to enter the lanes. Here are some key benefits of this system:

- **Congestion management**. Dynamic pricing helps manage congestion in the express lanes by adjusting toll rates in real time based on traffic conditions. Higher tolls during peak periods encourage some drivers to choose alternative routes or times, thus reducing congestion and improving traffic flow. In an emergency – late for an event or for picking up a child from daycare? – you get the choice of paying the additional dollars for the fast lane, knowing it will be sufficiently uncrowded to allow you to get there on time.
- **Reliable travel times**. By controlling the number of vehicles in the lanes through pricing, the lanes can maintain a consistent traffic flow, minimizing stop-and-go patterns and reducing the likelihood of unexpected delays. The result? More predictable and reliable travel times.
- **Improved carpooling and transit**. The strategy encourages carpooling and the use of public transport by incentivizing vehicles with multiple occupants. Carpoolers can use the express lanes toll-free, which helps reduce the number of single-occupancy vehicles on the road and promotes more sustainable and efficient transportation options.
- **Revenue generation**. The toll revenue generated can be reinvested into the transportation system for use in infrastructure improvements, maintenance, and future transportation projects. This helps to alleviate the strain on public budgets while supporting ongoing transportation initiatives.
- **Electric cars**. Electric vehicles (EVs) can use the lane at no additional charge, a benefit that has incentivized some to switch to EVs (and lower their carbon footprint).

Of course, the ideal is an infrastructure where traffic is better managed. While the traffic system in Atlanta has been scored as one
of the top 10 worst in the country, there is a body of opinion that
says that measures such as dynamic pricing lanes are only tem-
porary fixes. While useful in guiding the way to improved patterns
of use, the downside is that they can end up serving primarily as
a revenue-generation mechanism for governments, who then
have no incentive to improve their cities' infrastructure.

Key takeaways

As representatives of their citizens, governments are responsible for
environmental protection and societal welfare. How this mandate
translates into action can vary based on political affiliation and
policy ideology. This chapter has looked at the role of government
regulation in controlling pricing to achieve these ends.

- We have seen how taxes and tariffs can disincentivize negative
  behavior. Examples have ranged from tobacco in the U.S. to
  automobiles in Singapore. Subsidies are used to incentivize desirable behavior and usually work at an industry level. Examples
  are the agricultural subsidies used to regulate the supply side or
  the subsidies in the housing sector, which democratize housing
  and encourage sustainable building practices.
- Government pricing interventions also often manage the demand
  side of the equation. Tax credits and rebates can target consumers and, used effectively, can accelerate the adoption of solar
  panels. Norway presents a successful case where tax credits have
  massively boosted the adoption of EVs. Social messaging and
  non-price incentives can also accelerate the change. (We will
  have more to say about social norms in the next chapter.)
- Companies are not powerless here: they can (and frequently do)
  lobby the government to act as an agency for change. They must
  often rely on government support – via regulation or subsidies –
  to accelerate the adoption of pro-society initiatives to offset the
  associated higher costs.
- This chapter has also discussed several studies that explore
  the effects of price and other monetary incentives on health-
  promoting consumer behavior. We've seen how such fiscal mechanisms can dramatically increase the uptake of life-saving
  vaccines or improve dietary habits.
- The chapter has also examined two controversial areas of pricing
  interventions. Carbon pricing is an example of where putting a
  monetary value on pollution can have unintended consequences.

Insulin prices, as charged by pharmaceutical companies, show how the economic logic behind those companies' pricing strategies can sometimes backfire when confronted by social realities.

Notes

1 "What Is the Cost of Solar Panels in 2023?" Academic Gates, February 17, 2023. https://www.academicgates.com/news/story/what-is-the-cost-of-solar-panels-in-2023/17715

2 Julie Cart, "California's Residential Solar Rules Overhauled after Highly Charged Debate." Cal Matters, December 15, 2022. https://calmatters.org/environment/2022/12/california-solar-rules-overhauled

3 Internal Revenue Service, "Credits for New Electric Vehicles Purchased in 2022 or Before." June 22, 2023. https://www.irs.gov/credits-deductions/credits-for-new-electric-vehicles-purchased-in-2022-or-before

4 Chen Lin, "Singapore's Quirky Car Market Offers Rare Profit for Some as Prices Soar." *Reuters*, October 21, 2022. https://www.reuters.com/business/autos-transportation/singapores-quirky-car-market-offers-rare-profit-some-prices-soar-2022-10-21

5 Marco Bertini, Stefan Buehler, Daniel Halbheer, and Donald R Lehmann, "Review of Carbon Footprinting and Pricing under Climate Concerns." *Journal of Marketing* 86(2) (2022). https://doi.org/10.1177/0022242920932930

6 Lise Kingo, "Executive Update: Setting a $100 Price on Carbon." United Nations Global Compact, April 22, 2016. https://unglobalcompact.org/news/3361-04-22-2016

7 Johannes Urpelainen and Elisha George, "Reforming Global Fossil Fuel Subsidies: How the United States Can Restart International Cooperation." *Brookings*, July 14, 2021. https://www.brookings.edu/articles/reforming-global-fossil-fuel-subsidies-how-the-united-states-can-restart-international-cooperation

8 "Fossil Fuel Subsidies: A Closer Look at Tax Breaks and Societal Costs." Environmental and Energy Study Institute, July 29, 2019. https://www.eesi.org/papers/view/fact-sheet-fossil-fuel-subsidies-a-closer-look-at-tax-breaks-and-societal-costs

9 "Rally to End Fossil Fuel Subsidies in Washington D.C." Greenpeace Media, June 29, 2021. https://media.greenpeace.org/archive/Rally-to-End-Fossil-Fuel-Subsidies-in-Washington-D-C--27MDHUXWE6P.html

10 Ministry of Energy & Mineral Resources and Ministry of Finance, Republic of Indonesia, *Indonesia's Effort to Phase Out and Rationalise its Fossil-Fuel Subsidies*. 2019. https://www.oecd.org/fossil-fuels/publication/Indonesia%20G20%20Self-Report%20IFFS.pdf

11 "Let FHA Loans Help You." U.S. Department of Housing and Urban Development. https://www.hud.gov/buying/loans

12 "US Coronavirus Vaccine Tracker." USA Facts, May 3, 2023. https://usafacts.org/visualizations/covid-vaccine-tracker-states

13 Parsa Erfani and Margaret Bourdeux, *Can Vaccine Incentive Reward Programs Increase COVID-19 Vaccine Uptake?* Harvard Medical School,

Blavatnik Institute of Global Health and Social Medicine, 2022. https://ghsm.hms.harvard.edu/sites/default/files/assets/Programs/PublicPolicy/Vaccine%20Incentives_PGPPSC.pdf

14 John M. Yokley, David P. Fogleman, and Edward S. Shapiro. "A Lottery Program to Promote Childhood Immunization." *American Journal of Public Health* 74(7) (1984): 747–749.

15 G.S. Birkhead et al., "The Immunization of Children Enrolled in the Special Supplemental Food Program for Women, Infants, and Children (WIC): The Impact of Different Strategies." *Journal of the American Medical Association* 274(4) (July 1995): 312–316. https://pubmed.ncbi.nlm.nih.gov/7609260

16 Siobhan Gallagher, "Food Price Policy and Mortality: How to Even the Playing Field for Participants in SNAP." *Tufts Now*, May 16, 2018. https://now.tufts.edu/2018/05/16/food-price-policy-and-mortality-how-even-playing-field-participants-snap

17 Matthias Tay, "Subsidies for Food Operators Using Healthier Ingredients." Today Online, January 19, 2015. https://www.todayonline.com/singapore/subsidies-food-operators-using-healthier-ingredients

18 "Singapore's Health Promotion Board Emphasizes Whole Grain Options." Oldways Whole Grains Council, July 25, 2018. https://wholegrainscouncil.org/blog/2018/07/singapores-health-promotion-board-emphasizes-whole-grain-options

19 "Countries Share Examples of How Tobacco Tax Policies Create Win–Wins for Development, Health and Revenues." World Health Organization Newsroom, 2021. https://www.who.int/news-room/feature-stories/detail/countries-share-examples-of-how-tobacco-tax-policies-create-win-wins-for-development-health-and-revenues

20 "WHO Report on the Global Tobacco Epidemic 2021: Addressing New and Emerging Products." World Health Organization, July 27, 2021. https://www.who.int/publications/i/item/9789240032095

21 Karen Van Nuys, Erin Trish, and Neeraj Sood, "Who Is Really Driving up Insulin Costs?" USC Schaeffer, April 18, 2022. https://healthpolicy.usc.edu/article/who-is-really-driving-up-insulin-costs

22 Tara O'Neill Hayes and Katerina Kerska, "Agriculture Subsidies and Their Influence on the Composition of U.S. Food Supply and Consumption." American Action Forum, November 3, 2021. https://www.americanactionforum.org/research/primer-agriculture-subsidies-and-their-influence-on-the-composition-of-u-s-food-supply-and-consumption

23 "Water: The Right Price Can Encourage Efficiency and Investment." Organization for Economic Co-Operation and Development (OECD). https://www.oecd.org/env/resources/water-therightpricecanencourageefficiencyandinvestment.htm

6 Bringing customers along

> Our lives begin to end the day we become silent about
> things that matter.
>
> Martin Luther King Jr

"Bringing the customer along on the journey" is critical in ensuring a product or service's success. It is not enough to create a purpose-driven product; a company also needs first to encourage customers to buy it but also to make any behavioral changes that using the product entails. Take Tesla, for example. Merely creating a high-performing electric vehicle would not be enough on its own. The company had to educate customers about its superior performance and its positive environmental impact, as well as how to use an electric car. Moreover, customers had to adapt their behavior. They needed to know how to charge their vehicles – and where – and possibly also install a charging meter at home and get into the routine of charging it. They also show the savings over gas in their mobile app – hence continuously reinforcing the positive sensation of savings. It is not enough to produce it well, but priced affordably, and people should be able to use it and reuse it effectively.

A *Harvard Business Review* article[1] elaborates five ways to push customer behavior in the direction of sustainability, namely; harnessing social influence, cultivating positive habits, capitalizing on the domino effect, appealing to emotions and logic, and prioritizing experiences over ownership. The article emphasizes the importance of appealing not only to a consumer's rational side – making these behavioral changes easier to manage – but also to their social needs and wants and the emotional benefits (i.e., making customers feel good about the change). It is particularly when a new product or service requires a change of habit that the psychology of the consumer must be taken into account. In this chapter, we review some ways in which price can be used to incentivize customers toward pro-social behaviors.

Another *HBR* article[2] suggests helping companies manage product introductions that require behavioral change. For example,

DOI: 10.4324/9781032659008-8

Nike has launched a gender equality initiative. In the context of sports, the dropout rate for girls by age 14 is twice that of boys. Nike's "Made to Play" initiative aims to address this by collaborating with community partners to enhance girls' access to sports opportunities and recruit and train female coaches. Empowering women athletes requires more than just marketing: it requires merchandise. In this regard, Nike has put a lot of investment into developing girls' and women's sports gear, and generated a substantial revenue stream out of it: today, it accounts for about 25% of its total revenues, up from less than 10% in the 1990s. "Always," a female sanitary product provider, launched a campaign titled "Just Like a Girl," with the aim of encouraging girls to maintain their self-esteem during the vulnerable years of puberty and to develop a positive association with their product. Another effective way to engage consumers in a brand's sustainability agenda is to make the sustainable choice the easiest one. For example, Nespresso in Switzerland encourages recycling of its used coffee capsules by providing free packaging and home pickup through the postal service. In France, the retail chain Leclerc offers its customers "reusable, recyclable, and exchangeable for life" hessian (jute fabric) bags to facilitate the transition from plastic bags. Ongoing encouragement through incentives, positive feedback, and social inclusion serves to continue this partnership between companies and customers in pursuit of sustainability. Another important part of effecting successful transitions is building public awareness of the negative impacts of existing choices.

Why do people make pro-social choices?

Pro-social behavior is voluntary action intended to benefit another individual or group of individuals. Examples of actions that cost a person something in time or money but benefit others are helping someone in need, sharing valuable and limited resources, donating resources in the form of time or money, buying environmentally friendly products, paying taxes, and complying with social rules. Research confirms that people make pro-social choices primarily for two reasons: (1) *humans are naturally pro-social*; (2) *egocentrism*.[3] It is important for us to understand what motivates this behavior so we can leverage it for positive changes.

Humans are naturally pro-social

This is generally true for both humans and animals. For example, when a member of their kin is in danger, vervet monkeys emit calls to attract the predator.[4] Experiments have also shown that rats will sacrifice a reward to save other rats in danger. It is far from clear where the reasons for altruistic behavior lie, and there are competing theories.[5] But it can be readily observed in daily life. For example, a colleague of ours was traveling to New Zealand and had difficulty finding a parking space at the airport. It looked like she was going to miss her flight. The security line was long, and her flight was scheduled to depart in 30 minutes. But she made it because over 20 people in the line allowed her to jump ahead. Why did they do so when it gained them nothing and, in fact, only added to their own wait for security clearance? They would never meet our colleagues again. It is a clear case of altruism, but also possibly social norms or social pressure in action: once the first person ahead of her agreed to let her in, the rest followed suit.

Egocentrism

The second reason why humans make pro-social choices is egocentrism. This is where a person undertakes a pro-social action in order to accrue benefits to themselves either immediately or in the future. Expectations of *future reciprocity* can be either explicit or implicit, e.g., a card you can redeem at a later date.[6] Pro-social actions can also confer *self-esteem, social inclusiveness*, and feel-good/*positive feelings*.[7] Donating to a good cause or helping in a soup kitchen can leave you feeling good about yourself. It represents a personal motivation for pro-social action.

Pricing strategies to stimulate pro-social behavior

Having looked at why people make pro-social decisions, we now examine the role that price plays in persuading people to make pro-social decisions. For example, reusable shopping bags are an eco-friendly alternative to single-use plastic bags, which use materials that contribute to plastic waste. Reusable bags can also be money-saving for retailers, who have previously provided single-use bags for free. Currently, most stores offer reusable bags at a small purchase price, to encourage sale, they are often priced low or given away for free at events. However, buyers leave them at home or in their car and get their groceries bagged in the usual plastic or paper bags. Sprouts, a U.S. grocery store, recently started charging 10 cents for a single-use grocery bag, a small fee but an inducement to many to return to the car and fetch the reusable bag. Similarly, the grocery store Fresh Market charges customers 5 cents for plastic bags and 20 cents for paper ones, also creating a revenue stream for the retailer in addition to motivating sustainable behavior.

Are there other ways to induce this behavior? For example, retailers could provide incentives, such as discounts or loyalty points, for customers who regularly bring their reusable bags? To effect this behavior shift, *the retailer is can to implement a four-pronged approach*:

- Educate customers on why plastic bags are bad for the environment.
- Provide incentives to buy a reusable bag. They must be readily available and at an affordable price or else given for free after a minimum purchase amount.
- Create incentives to use reusable bags on subsequent occasions. These could be: a donation to a charity; a contribution to planting a tree; money back; or loyalty points.
- Create a disincentive to use paper or plastic bags, for example by levying a small charge.

A four-pronged approach is needed to maximize the opportunity for behavior change and form new habits. To change consumer behavior in pro-social directions, companies must be strategic when it comes to their marketing communications and pay attention to research into behavioral factors. Customers need to be educated about the product and its benefits to society, as well as how to use it.

Social interventions and purpose-driven pricing

In this section, we will explore and build on ideas around social interventions. Based on research, these can be applied in practice with the ultimate goal of improving social and environmental outcomes. To begin with, we draw on the work of Kahneman and apply a pricing-for-purpose lens.

Create financial disincentives to discourage a continuation of damaging behavior

Loss aversion is a cognitive bias that describes people's tendency to avoid a loss rather than acquire a gain of equal value. In other words, people tend to experience the pain of losing something more strongly than the pleasure of gaining something. The concept of loss aversion was first proposed by psychologists Amos Tversky and Daniel Kahneman in 1991 as part of their research on behavioral economics and decision-making.[8] They found that people are more likely to take risks to avoid a loss than they are to achieve a gain, even if the potential outcomes amount to the same in value.

This cognitive bias can affect many areas of life, including financial decision-making, investing, and personal relationships. For example, a person may be more willing to hold onto a losing investment in the hope that it will eventually recover than she is to sell it and accept the loss. Loss aversion can also be seen in everyday situations, such as when someone is reluctant to part with a possession with sentimental value or hesitant to switch to a new product or service, even though it could save them money or improve their quality of life. Recognizing the influence of loss aversion on decision-making can help individuals and organizations make informed choices and avoid making decisions based solely on emotional reactions to potential losses.

Loss aversion can have significant implications for pricing strategies in a range of contexts. Sprout's decision to charge a mere ten cents for the paper shopping bag, rather than continue to offer it for free is an example of how loss aversion can be implemented. Earlier in the book, we talked about increasing the price of goods and services with poor environmental and social credentials. What needs to be factored in here is that, when it comes to prices, consumers tend to be more sensitive to losses than they are to gains. If a product is priced too high, consumers may perceive the large financial sacrifice as a loss, which deters them from purchasing. If a product is discounted, consumers may perceive the savings as a gain, motivating them to buy even if they don't need it. On the other hand, if a company initially prices a product low and then increases it, consumers may perceive the increase as a loss and be less willing to purchase.

Case: Shifting consumer behavior to save water

To take a case from Turkey, the dishwashing detergent brand Finish launched a campaign under the slogan "Save water for tomorrow" in order to promote a shift in consumer behavior. Turkey is set to face severe water shortages by 2030; if consumption patterns don't change, things could be dire. Reckitt, the company that manufactures Finish, discovered that half of Turkish households rinsed dishes before placing them in the dishwasher, resulting in significant water use. Its Finish Quantum detergent is specifically formulated for the purpose of directly placing dishes in the dishwasher, and its "Skip the rinse" campaign educated consumers about the benefits of doing so – a water saving of up to 57 liters per load. Concurrently, Reckitt partnered with media companies, dishwasher manufacturers, and Turkish water departments to *raise awareness and encourage consumers* to contemplate the prospects of the next generation facing water shortages. These initiatives not only increased brand awareness and reversed market-share losses but also reduced water usage by 20%.[9]

Create incentives to reward pro-social behaviors

A study in the *Journal of Business Ethics* suggests that customers will likely not trade the functional benefits of a product for hedonic value.[10] This is particularly true for products in which performance is critical, such as running shoes or cleaning supplies. But in products that perform worse than – or at least are perceived to be inferior to – competing products, altruistic feelings or feelings of social belonging can be tapped into to encourage pro-social action. The rewards and incentives can take the form of a sense of belonging to an exclusive group or of being a good citizen. Customers are encouraged to make a purchase by a 'feelgood' sense of giving back to the community. In all cases, the emotional and psychological value of the product must be strong for a switch to occur and be sustained.

A popular Corporate Social Responsibility (CSR) campaign involved Procter & Gamble's Pampers branded diapers. For every packet of Pampers purchased, one vaccine was donated to UNICEF in their drive to eliminate maternal and neonatal tetanus. In many places around the world, women typically deliver babies in their homes, occasionally in conditions lacking proper sanitation. Without adequate protection from tetanus, the lives of both mother and child are at risk. This is a good example of alignment: Pampers are products for babies, and expectant mothers are the recipients of the vaccinations. Similarly, Yoplait had a campaign in which it donates to the Susan G. Komen Foundation, an organization that raises awareness of and researches breast cancer. Again, the alignment makes sense because the demographic of the yogurt buyers is predominantly female. Donations to this cause will more likely be triggered by altruism. The relationship between the cost of the donations and the benefit is an essential consideration here. The donations are a cost for the manufacturers, but, more often, they create price inelasticity in the minds of consumers related to the cause. In other words, customers are willing to pay more and less likely to switch to a cheaper product.

Social interventions can be an effective way of encouraging engagement with a brand, and these are factored into both marketing and pricing. For example, for every pair of shoes purchased, TOMS donates one pair of shoes to a child in Ethiopia.[11] Similarly, the fast-food restaurant chain Wendy's launched a US$2 key tag supporting the Dave Thomas Foundation for Adoption. In return for signing up, customers receive a free Jr. Frosty with every food purchase for the remainder of the year. *Customer relationship management messages can appeal either to consumers' self-benefits (egocentric impulses) or to altruistic benefits.* In these cases, whereas the TOMS campaign message appeals to consumers' altruism, Wendy's was targeted at customers' egocentric drives.

There are a lot of companies currently engaging in these types of *cause-related marketing* initiatives. In 2018, North American spending on corporate sponsorship overall was $24.2 billion. Of this, 9% was dedicated to worthy causes, totaling $2.14 billion in 2018 and expected to be $4 billion in 2023.[12]

"Framing" is an important aspect of cause-related marketing and social interventions. For example, companies might see their CSR obligations as requiring them to offer a percentage of revenue to charity, which acts as indirect marketing for their products or services. However, social interventions must be tailored to different customers. Socio-economic status, education, and so on can all affect how a customer processes the marketing of social interventions.

Many retail stores and businesses implement a practice called "rounding up" or "round up to donate" at the point of sale to encourage customers to contribute to charitable causes. The practice of "rounding up" to donate is a form of "checkout charity" or "point of sale giving." It's a relatively simple way for retailers to facilitate charitable giving by customers, making it easy for people to contribute small amounts that, when combined, can have a meaningful impact on important causes. Additionally, it can enhance a store's reputation by demonstrating a commitment to social responsibility and community engagement. The social pressure to donate a small amount when the cashier and people in line are watching is an effective framing of the donation request. Donating an additional 56 cents seems small compared to an overall bill of $85.44.

The warning about greenwashing

Greenwashing refers to the practice of disseminating inaccurate or deceptive information about the environmental advantages of a product or activity. Companies might maintain or even ramp up their polluting and harmful practices while exploiting the trust and good intentions of environmentally conscious consumers. Greenwashing can be thought of as the imbalance between a firm's actual pro-environmental efforts and its public claims. The term was coined in 1986 by Jay Westerveld, an American environmentalist. During his visit to the Beachcomber Resort in Fiji, he noticed signs asking customers to *reuse the towels because the oceans and reefs are important, and these efforts would help preserve them*. While reusing towels might contribute in a small way to reducing environmental impact, the resort was planning to expand into other parts of the island, with coral reefs suffering collateral damage. In light of this, pro-environment messages about towels look like a cynical attempt to deceive and deflect.

It is ultimately a lack of coordination between a business's functions that ends up leaving them facing charges of greenwashing. Firms such as Coca-Cola, H&M, Mercedes Benz, and Volkswagen have all endured the negative publicity of accusations of greenwashing because of a disjointed approach.[13] As companies embark on marketing activities that make claims about their products, they need to be authentic and internally aligned.

These days, firms are cautious about publicizing their positive endeavors for fear of backlash. Indeed, they need to be mindful of the issue of "perceived fairness," which is critical for strategies dependent on consumer participation. If customers perceive that the brand is shifting the burden of its sustainability agenda onto them while remaining inactive, they are likely to resist. The key message here in relation to pricing is: that unless customers buy into the idea that a company is genuine in its societal commitments, they will not pay the price premium. Even companies with strong "purpose-driven" reputations can get into trouble and undo the work they have done in building their image. The U.S. supermarket chain Whole Foods Markets, for example, has faced intense scrutiny due to allegations of overpricing and mislabeling when New York City's Department of Consumer Affairs Commissioner unveiled findings from an investigation in 2015. The investigation revealed a pattern of overcharging customers by inflating the stated weight of pre-packaged meat, dairy, and baked goods in the chain's stores. Whole Foods paid a fine of US$500,000 and suffered severe damage to its pricing reputation.[14] Also in 2015, a customer in California found a bottle that contained just three stalks of asparagus in water at one of the stores priced at $5.99 and posted it on Instagram, deriding it. The post made it onto the news channels, forcing Whole Foods to remove the items from its shelves.[15] Customers were outraged since a bunch of asparagus costs $5, and having just three in a bottle with tap water at $5.99 felt unfair to the customers. The customers found no health benefits associated with asparagus water, and it was something created by the company that caused even more distrust for the product and price fairness perception.

So, when developing incentives/disincentives for certain customer behaviors being authentic and aligned with internal organizational departments is important.

The high price of free

Many non-governmental organizations (NGOs) and government agencies will provide products and services free of charge to the community. Such organizations might be mission-philanthropic and/or funded by donations or tax dollars and are not, in fact, oriented to exact payments. However, we aim to show you that organizations that give away goods at no cost may be better off charging a small fee.

When something is offered "free," a psychological response is triggered. This is a frequent area of study for behavioral economists. Here is an example using an experiment with chocolate.[16] The researchers gave students the option to purchase a Lindt Truffle for 26 cents or a Hershey's Kiss for 1 cent. Some 40% of the participants chose the truffle, while another 40% chose the Kiss. But when they lowered the price of both chocolates by just 1 cent, they noticed a significant behavior change: 90% of participants opted for the free Kiss, even though the price difference remained the same. They concluded that the word "free" is powerful – a force to be reckoned with. The researchers mainly ascribed this phenomenon to the "certainty" effect: if it turned out to be not as good, the buyer's remorse was minimal, not having parted with any cash. Furthermore, as well as instinctively choosing the "free" option, we tend to overconsume free items even when they're not suitable for us. Charging for something will not only guide better purchasing, but also helps to manage how much of it we consume.

Next, we present a case in which charging a nominal price for a service is shown to be better than giving it away for free.

Case: The Al-Azhar Park, Cairo

In this case, we explore the importance of charging a nominal price – rather than allowing free access – for sustaining and maintaining community resources such as parks and libraries.

A public–private partnership, Al-Azhar Park in Cairo, Egypt, is a noteworthy public park that has earned several distinctions, including being named one of the world's top 60 public spaces by the Project for Public Spaces. This popular tourist destination is located between historic old Cairo, containing a wealth of important medieval Islamic monuments and the City of the Dead, and provides excellent views of the surrounding area.

The 30-hectare (74-acre) park was established on Al-Darassa by the Aga Khan Trust for Culture (AKTC), following a decision in 1984 by His Highness the Aga Khan to donate a park to the people of Cairo. The park's western side is adjacent to the old Fatimid city and its extension, Al-Darb Al-Ahmar, which boasts numerous mosques, madrasas, and mausoleas marked by a line of minarets. The Mosque-Madrasa of Sultan Hassan and the Ayyubid Citadel are to the south, while the eastern side overlooks the City of the Dead, an area densely populated with social welfare complexes sponsored by Mamluk sultans and dignitaries. Cairo, one of the densest cities in the world, is notable for its lack of green public spaces; the park provides the citizens of Cairo a much-needed space for respite and relaxation. Its hilly topography, formed by centuries of debris, offers elevated viewpoints with a spectacular 360-degree panorama of the historic Cairo townscape. Two key considerations in the park's development were (a) economic impact and (b) environmental sustainability.[17]

- **Economic impact**. An important factor was *community involvement*. This meant that local small and medium-sized businesses are supported, jobs created, and *local artistic talent was nurtured*. The development has also improved the value of *real estate* in the area. According to Susan Wachter, co-director at the University of Pennsylvania's Penn Institute for Urban Research, "Creating parks substantially raises the desirability of an area and the amount people are willing to pay to live in surrounding properties."[18]
- **Environmental sustainability**. Being the largest green space developed in Cairo in over a century, the park serves as a green "lung" for the city. To ensure its environmental sustainability – taking into account the context of a water supply crisis in Cairo and the local hot, dry climate – it has an advanced irrigation system for its vast open spaces, which uses minimal volumes of water. A large lake has been constructed in the style of classic Islamic parks, further adding to its magnificence. Water from nearby underground reservoirs is used to supply it, which avoids the need for long pipes, keeping costs down and also preserving valuable water resources. A nursery was established off-site during the design and construction of the park so that trees and plants could be tested and selected based on their adaptability to the soil conditions and climate.

The pricing dilemma: whether or not to charge an entrance fee

The long-run financial sustainability of NGO-sponsored projects is often challenging, and governments often struggle to find the resources to maintain their investment. Al-Azhar Park therefore chose to charge an entrance fee to visitors. The cost varies by day of the week, ranging between 40 and 45 Egyptian pounds (roughly equivalent to US$1.25–1.50). Other sources of revenue include the park's two restaurants, events, and various kiosks.

Although the entrance fees and other revenue go into maintaining the park, the fee structure nevertheless came under criticism, being seen as unaffordable for many Cairo residents. With the park being a valuable resource for local residents for recreation, relaxation, and social gatherings, this triggered an important debate about whether or not public spaces such as these should be available for free.

We looked for evidence at similar urban green spaces that had allowed free access. In many cases, we noted that they had become havens for illegal activities. Plus, they deteriorated through a lack of maintenance. The result was an undesirable area, losing its popularity among residents, with the outcome being the loss of the green space altogether. There are two prime examples of this in Cairo itself. Built in 1989 on a 105-hectare site, Fustat Garden provided a much-needed green space. Never intended as a high-end, sophisticated destination, it was earmarked as an urban green space created for the general public to relax. However, its popularity was ultimately its downfall. With a lack of management, it became a venue for undesirable activity. It has low levels of security and is seen as unsafe for local residents. The Giza Zoo, constructed in 1891, met with a similar fate. Its variety of animals, beautiful green areas, and cheap entrance fees made it attractive to Egyptians of all socio-economic levels. However, its popularity was its undoing as well. A large number of daily visitors – over 250,000 at one point – led to a decline in the natural environment within the zoo. Open spaces had to be converted into pathways and seating areas in order to accommodate all the visitors. Additionally, the entrance fee was too low to generate the funds to sufficiently maintain it and keep it clean. An entrance fee serves more than one purpose. For one, it is a demand management tool to ensure the long-term viability of the park by controlling numbers. And second, it is a means of making the park financially sustainable and keeping it clean, secure, and appealing. The surpluses from park revenue are used to fund social and economic development programs in the adjoining Darb al-Ahmar neighborhood. There are other benefits to society:

1. There is a positive impact on air quality throughout Cairo. The park is often referred to as the "lungs" of Cairo as it raises the quality of outdoor spaces throughout the city.
2. In addition to the jobs created by the park itself, community revitalization and increased economic activity are evident in the area surrounding the park. Local handicrafts have flourished, and age-old artistic traditions are maintained.
3. It is one of the top tourist destinations in Cairo, which brings in more shoppers buying local traditional goods.
4. By charging an entrance fee, you create a sense of civic responsibility. For instance, in Azhar Park, visitors throw their garbage in bins. Outside the park, people discard their trash on the streets.

The model has proven so effective that the Egyptian Government is building similar parks around Cairo. There are good examples of other public spaces that are well-maintained and sustainable because they charge a nominal fee. Jogger's Park, a small park in the Bandra suburb of Mumbai, and the National Zoo in Kenya both charge an entrance fee, which ensures their long-term sustainability and makes them financially self-sufficient, not drawing on public funds.

The U.S. National Park Service charges a $10–$35 entrance fee per vehicle at 109 out of over 400 parks. However, it may be a victim of its own success. Because its parks are well maintained, more people want to visit. One suggestion is a dynamic pricing model based on demand, with higher prices charged in summer. This argument has been made by Margaret A. Walls, a research director and senior fellow at Resources for the Future in Washington, DC. In 2016, U.S. National Parks celebrated their 100th anniversary and marked it by allowing free entrance to all the parks. The number of visitors sky-rocketed, which led to overcrowding in many sites. Also, parks are beginning to restrict access to control pollution and congestion. But this has led to long waiting times to get in, parking congestion, and oversubscribed lodging. A differentiated fee structure can help with park maintenance. "That might mean a zero, or very low, cost during some seasons at some parks, but it means a significantly higher fee at the most popular parks during the summer months."[18] Many parks have a backlog of maintenance projects – bridges, roads, water and sewer systems, and so on. These projects are essential in keeping parks safe for future generations, and charging a fee can create a revenue stream to fund these projects. It's clear that entrance fees represent a better long-term strategy.

Key takeaways

In this chapter, we have discussed the importance of "bringing the customer along on the journey" when it comes to pro-social actions. This means engaging with customers' behavior before and after purchase.

- Consumer behavioral psychology, as well as the context of social and cultural norms, both need to be understood and evaluated in order to create strategies that can incentivize customers to change their buying habits.
- We have emphasized the role of pricing in facilitating behavior change. A multi-pronged approach is recommended to accelerate change and create social impact, with price being a critical

lever. For example, charging for grocery bags to incent buyers to bring reusable bags and as a disincentive to use plastic bags.

• We have also explored the dilemma of whether to charge a fee or whether to grant free access to public resources such as parks. We conclude that a nominal entrance fee ensures the long-term viability and sustainability of high-demand public spaces.

Notes

1 Katherine White, David J. Hardisty, and Rishad Habib, "The Elusive Green Consumer." *Harvard Business Review*, July–August 2019.
2 Goutam Challegalla and Frédéric Dalsace, "Moving the Needle on Sustainability." *Harvard Business Review Magzine*, November–December 2022. https://hbr.org/2022/11/moving-the-needle-on-sustainability
3 D. Findley-Van Nostrand and T. Ojanen, "Forms of Prosocial Behaviors are Differentially Linked to Social Goals and Peer Status in Adolescents." *Journal of Genetic Psychology* 179(6) (November–December 2018): 329–342. https://doi.org/10.1080/00221325.2018.1518894
4 Brigit Katz, "Green Monkeys Borrow Their Cousins' Eagle Warning Call When Drones Are Near." *Smithsonian Magazine*, May 29, 2019. https://www.smithsonianmag.com/smart-news/when-confronted-scary-drones-green-monkeys-emit-alarm-call-eagles-180972302
5 C.D. Batson, "Prosocial Motivation: Is It Ever Truly Altruistic?" In L. Berkowitz (ed.), *Advances in Experimental Social Psychology*, Vol. 20 (Academic Press, 1987): 65–122.
  C.D. Batson, *Altruism in Humans* (Oxford University Press, 2011).
6 J. Andreoni, "Impure Altruism and Donations to Public Goods: A Theory of Warm-glow Giving." *The Economic Journal* 100(401) (1990): 464–477. https://doi.org/10.2307/2234133
  R.B. Cialdini, *Influence: The Psychology of Persuasion* (HarperCollins, 1987).
7 L.B. Aknin, E.W. Dunn, and M.I. Norton, "Happiness Runs in a Circular Motion: Evidence for a Positive Feedback Loop between Prosocial Spending and Happiness." *Journal of Happiness Studies* 13(2) (2012): 347–355. https://psycnet.apa.org/doi/10.1007/s10902-011-9267-5
  A. Imas, "The Effect of Charity Choice on Social Signaling and Giving." *Journal of Economic Behavior & Organization* 106 (2014): 409–422. https://doi.org/10.1016/j.jebo.2014.07.007
  U. Khan, K. Goldsmith, and R. Dhar, "Don't Stop Believing: Rituals Improve Performance by Decreasing Anxiety." *Organizational Behavior and Human Decision Processes* 161 (2020): 46–62. https://doi.org/10.1016/j.obhdp.2020.04.002
8 A. Tversky and D. Kahneman, "Loss Aversion in Riskless Choice: A Reference-Dependent Model." *Quarterly Journal of Economics* 106(4) (November 1991): 1039–1061. https://doi.org/10.2307/2937956
9 Goutam Challagalla and Frédéric Dalsace, "Moving the Needle on Sustainability." *Harvard Business Review Magazine*, November–December 2022. https://hbr.org/2022/11/moving-the-needle-on-sustainability

10 Michael G. Luchs and Minu Kumar, "'Yes, but this Other One Looks Better/Works Better': How Do Consumers Respond to Trade-offs between Sustainability and Other Valued Attributes?" *Journal of Business Ethics* 140(3) (February 2017): 567–584. https://www.jstor.org/stable/44164311

11 K. White and J. Peloza, "Self-Benefit versus Other-benefit Marketing Appeals: Their Effectiveness in Generating Charitable Donations." *Journal of Marketing* 73(4) (2009): 109–124. https://doi.org/10.1509/jmkg.73.4.109

12 IEG, *What Sponsors Want and Where Dollars Will Go in 2018*. IEG Sponsorship Report, 2018. http://www.sponsorship.com/IEG/files/f3/f3cfac41-2983-49be-8df6-3546345e27de.pdf

"Top Cause Marketing Statistics in 2023." Amra & Elma. https://www.amraandelma.com/cause-marketing-statistics

13 Truth in Advertising.org, "Companies Accused of Greenwashing." April 22, 2022, updated October 27, 2023. https://truthinadvertising.org/articles/companies-accused-greenwashing

14 Lisa Hale, "Angry Whole Foods Forced To Pay $500k Fine To Stop Pricing Investigation." *Inquisitr*, December 29, 2015. https://www.inquisitr.com/2664511/angry-whole-foods-forced-to-pay-500000-fine

15 Jennifer Earl, "Whole Foods Removes $6 'Asparagus Water' from Shelves." CBS News, August 4, 2015. https://www.cbsnews.com/news/whole-foods-removes-6-asparagus-water-from-store-shelves

16 N. Mazar, K. Shampanier, and D. Ariely, "When Retailing and Las Vegas Meet: Probabilistic Free Price Promotions." *Management Science*, Forthcoming. Rotman School of Management Working Paper No. 2636093 (March 10, 2016). https://ssrn.com/abstract=2636093

17 AKTC (2004) "Cairo, Revitalising a Historic Metropolis," Umberto Allemandi & C., Turin, Italy. AKTC (2004), "Al-Azhar Park Program Brief, Historic Cities Support Program," Geneva, Switzerland.

18 "The Park of a Thousand Pieces." *The Pennsylvania Gazette*, 1 July 2011. https://thepenngazette.com/the-park-of-a-thousand-pieces

Margaret A. Walls, "Protecting Our National Parks: New Entrance Fees Can Help." *Resources*, September 14, 2016. https://www.resources.org/archives/protecting-our-national-parks-new-entrance-fees-can-help

7   Ecosystems of collaborators

Chuck Davenport and Alpa Sutaria

If you want to go fast, go alone. If you want to go far, go together.

African Proverb

The sustainability continuum

How does a company transform into an organization with purpose? A purpose journey can begin simply with a one-off project or a charity initiative. It can ultimately extend as far as getting its entire supply chain to be purpose-driven.

The motivations for embarking on such a journey can vary. They can come from internal leadership goals or pressure from employees (younger generations, especially, are less willing to tolerate environmentally irresponsible behavior from the firms they work for). And they can come from external pressures: from customers and supply chain partners, from the competition, or from investors.

Even though they might not explicitly be aware of it, when it comes to sustainability, every company lies somewhere along the Sustainability Continuum (see Figure 7.1). At one end is "Denial": firms are avoiding the topic of sustainability and taking no action around it. Then comes "Deferral": they are still waiting to act, constrained by a lack of resources in terms of personnel or funding. Next is "Defense": firms are reactive, responding to pressures (legislative, shifting consumer values) as they come along; they feel the need to protect their existing business models. By playing "Offense," firms are proactive, anticipating trends and aiming to be strategic. Finally, a firm can achieve "Transformation" by leading its industry through its commitments and actions. Ultimately, a company's position on this continuum predicts the actions that it will take to drive sustainable outcomes and the solutions it seeks.

Whatever first motivates a firm to begin the sustainability journey, the Sustainability Continuum is an important benchmark to measure progress along that journey.

DOI: 10.4324/9781032659008-9

SUSTAINABILITY CONTINUUM

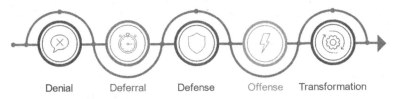

Denial   Deferral   Defense   Offense   Transformation

Figure 7.1 The Sustainability Continuum.
Source: WestRock Company.

Barriers to transformation

Below, we briefly describe barriers to progress along the Sustainability Continuum. Much of the literature on market penetration and growth focuses on business-to-consumer (B2C) firms, but in this chapter, we will talk a lot about the supply chain and, therefore, the business-to-business (B2B) market. A firm taking the sustainability path has an obligation to bring its suppliers along the journey with it if it is going to make a meaningful difference. Partnering, collaborating, and educating the suppliers in the ecosystem will be crucial to long-term success, especially bearing in mind that not all suppliers will be at the same stage when it comes to sustainability objectives. Furthermore, the circular economy (more on this below) has created new markets with new market dynamics that need regulation and quality control and introduce pricing opportunities.

Our research looked at barriers from an internal perspective. We found four primary obstacles facing B2B firms' adoption and expansion of sustainable practices and hence their progress along the Sustainability Continuum.

1. Motivation
2. Knowledge
3. Availability of resources
4. Affordability

Each of these barriers requires different solutions. For example, improving the availability of recycled material requires improved collaboration and cooperation with partners along the value chain; improving the performance on affordability may require product redesign, which, in turn, may need a complete change of supply chain partners or new monetization models and pricing strategies. In exploring these barriers, insights are afforded into obstacles facing suppliers making their way along the path to "circularity." The circular economy has exciting future growth potential as a route toward true sustainability for industrial systems.

We will now look at each of the four barriers in turn.

Motivation

As discussed earlier, a company can embark on its journey for a range of reasons: economic, altruistic, existential. Pressure can come from customers, competition, leadership, employees, or government regulation. We will take an example from the plastics ecosystem as a case study. In February 2019, Walmart announced aggressive targets for recycled packaging content on its shelves, which went as follows:

- Seek to achieve 100% recyclable, reusable, or industrially compostable packaging for its private brand packaging by 2025.
- Target at least 20% post-consumer recycled content in private brand packaging by 2025.
- Label 100% of food and consumable private brand packaging with the How2Recycle® label by 2022.
- Work with suppliers to eliminate the non-recyclable material PVC in general merchandise packaging by 2020.
- Reduce private-brand plastic packaging when possible, optimizing the use to meet the need.[1]

These goals represent significant movement toward reducing the carbon footprint of packaging. But Walmart has a history of bold initiatives involving its suppliers. Its mandates on RFID (radio-frequency identification) tagging were sweeping, but Walmart could not fully drive the initiative alone: it took the Covid-19 crisis and other business pressures to bring costs and technology performance into a range where broad implementation is feasible. Similarly, Walmart's goals are a step toward better circularity, but it can't achieve this by mandate alone. Only operational and financial feasibility throughout the value chain will enable sustainable progress.

On the other end of the supply chain, some of the world's largest plastics manufacturers are making their own commitments. Here are some examples:

- LyondellBasell, a Netherlands multinational chemical company, announced its intention to sell 2 million metric tons of recycled and renewable polymers by 2030.[2]
- Saudi chemical manufacturing company SABIC has committed to 1 million metric tons of circular production by 2030.[3]
- U.S. multinational corporation Dow Inc. has expanded its previous goal of an annual 1 million metric tons of circular and renewable plastics to three million.[4]

These commitments, representing both ends of the value chain for plastic consumer packaging, have significant motivation and have demonstrated sufficient knowledge and awareness of the issues. Walmart, by far the largest retailer by retail sales, is in a unique position to demand progress – and indeed, therefore, has a significant responsibility to do so. Similarly, the large plastics producers are feeding a still-increasing demand for their products, but there is growing concern over their impact, and this must be felt by the producers themselves. However, ethical motivations are in themselves potentially insufficient for acting at scale if supply dynamics and economic incentives are not aligned. Explicit demand from the value chain for a shift from traditional materials to recycled materials, however, is a powerful motivating force.

A model of failure...and success

The utility industry has been facing a similar set of challenges while working on a transition away from fossil fuel-based generation. Although green energy projects might theoretically seem a good bet, with the inputs – wind and solar – being free, capital sources saw the projects as higher risk and demanded higher interest rates. A unilateral effort by the utilities themselves to build renewable capacity achieved little other than increasing their cost of generation and taking capital budgets away from "proven" technologies. As public sentiment gravitated toward cleaner solutions, demand for green energy increased, opening the door for new economic arrangements and green energy tariffs and tax credits. This enabled utilities to charge differentiated rates on an "opt-in" basis for "pure" green energy. For example, AEP Ohio customers residing in Columbus have been automatically enrolled in the Clean Energy Columbus Program, an initiative that transitions their energy sources to clean energy supplied by AEP Energy.

Instead of co-mingling the costs of fossil-fuel-based and green energy, the industry created a new class of products for which customers would pay a premium. The result was significant growth in green energy generation and, over time, a significant reduction in the cost per kilowatt-hour of green energy. This new economic arrangement helped solve the capital supply issue by enabling evidence to emerge for the project's economic feasibility. It also solved energy supply problems thanks to improved technologies and project experience. Additionally, it is now also helping solve demand issues, as the cost of green energy in many places is below that of traditional generation. The key lesson to be learned here is that if we want broad-scale, sustainable shifts across an industry, the entire supply and demand chains need to work together toward an economically positive solution for all constituencies. Furthermore, government incentives are not a trivial factor in the success of many of the technologies. Just as the U.S. Energy Policy Acts of 1975, 1978, 1992, and 2005 significantly affected baseline technology development and demand creation, similar support may be needed to help accelerate the collection of renewable feedstocks to provide fodder for additional circularity capacity. NextEra was able to use governmental support, and, in 2021, the vast majority of the electricity generated by their facilities came from a diverse blend of clean and renewable sources, such as wind, solar, combined-cycle natural gas, and nuclear energy. For example, in the case of food and beverage manufacturer Chemlife (name anonymized), its profits are steady, and its customers are satisfied. However, in a recent meeting with the executive team, the CEO asked if they should consider environmental sustainability and energy needs and whether these might impact their business in the future. Making changes to chemical manufacturing facilities to improve the environmental profile and switch to renewable energy sources requires a significant financial investment in R&D and new talent. At what point, if at all, should they make the switch? Only when either the funding is there or else the external pressures, such as customer demand, reach a tipping point does it become easier for firms to justify embarking on the journey.

Firms in the "Denial" stage of the Sustainability Continuum are often faced with such a dilemma and continue business as usual without taking the next step. This accurately describes Kodak, the photographic company that saw the digital revolution coming but failed to respond. Its investments in photographic paper plants were considerable, so it chose to remain in denial about the paradigm shift that the digital revolution was about to usher in. However, when faced with emerging competition from innovation or changing customer expectations, companies often play "Defense" out of an understandable desire to protect existing competitive and business models, revenue, and profit streams – especially when built on large-scale manufacturing and commercial infrastructure.

Disrupting these models requires the conviction that the cost of doing nothing (i.e., not changing) is higher than the cost of switching.

Take the famous example of Toyota in the 1970s. When the leading carmakers worldwide saw the idea of building "quality" into their production processes as an added cost, the Toyota model was born. In this model, the entire lifecycle of cars – from design to materials procurement to manufacturing and delivery – was designed to incorporate quality. And, in fact, rather than increasing costs, it created one of the world's most-studied manufacturing and supply chain models. It generated enviable customer loyalty and boasted a dominant market share for decades.

Knowledge

The journey to becoming a purpose-driven organization can be long and tedious. Although there are famous case studies of companies in the vanguard – such as Unilever, Nike, and Chipotle – the majority of the companies across different industries will have different experiences. There are plenty of B2B and B2C firms still determining their role and the timing of their path forward. When, where, and how should we invest in the area? Or will it be better to wait? At this stage, it can be a lack of knowledge that presents the biggest challenge. Companies can easily get stuck in the "Deferral" stage. Recent studies have shown that while companies, both large and small, have committed to embracing the circular economy and signing up for various environmental sustainability objectives, most need help developing pathways to actually deliver on these commitments. The challenges are wide-ranging. Considerations around the evolving landscape of the circular economy, in particular, can be complex. Organizations such as the Ellen MacArthur Foundation and The Recycling Partnership can offer helpful advice. These organizations are on the leading edge of circular-economy solutions.

Availability

The availability of recycled materials in sufficient quantities is a limiting factor in scaling up to allow mass penetration of environmentally sustainable offerings. The supply of materials is inconsistent, which can result in production disruptions and machine downtimes. Addressing this by storing materials increases inventory costs. Additionally, the quality of recycled materials also fluctuates and is unlikely to meet desired standards consistently. The result is inconsistent products or a need to redesign manufacturing to integrate the new materials. Quantity and quality of materials are both relevant issues. Take the example of high-quality recycled PET (polyethylene terephthalate – the most common polymer resin used in fibers for clothing, containers for liquids, and foods). The recycling rate for PET is notoriously low across the U.S. and, indeed, in many parts of the world. Due to increasing pressure on companies to use less virgin plastic and increase their use of recycled plastics, many beverage manufacturers have committed to objectives around recycling and recycled content – so much so that the supply of food-grade recycled PET is projected to run short of company needs by 2024/25. A steady, high-quality supply of recycled PET can only come from collected, sorted, cleaned, and processed PET.[5] The scale supply chain for this is still being created. To develop it, beverage manufacturers are investing heavily in ecosystems with PET producers, recyclers, waste management companies, and others.

Affordability

When discussing the affordability of environmentally preferable materials, two issues typically arise. First, when materials are available, the price might be such that they would not be profitable; even if the high prices were passed along, the customer would not be willing to pay. Second, developing an eco-friendly product can require significant and costly investment. The question of "who pays?" arises at this stage. Both these issues can put a brake on efforts to be environmentally sustainable. Consumers increasingly expect products to include sustainability considerations (organic, recycled, recyclable, compostable, reusable, fair trade, etc.). In years past, such expectations were more in the minority, and companies could find a niche of consumers willing to pay more for products with environmental benefits. Today, what was once a "premium" offering is now becoming a requirement. With consumers less willing to pay the environmental premium, the burden falls on the suppliers and across the value chain. For example, when General Mills wants 100% recycled packaging – the responsible solution but at the same price – the onus is on the packaging manufacturing companies, cutting into their profits. Cost engineering – the management of project cost – becomes a critical part of the growth of the firm. We discuss cost engineering, also known as target costing, in Chapter 3.

Stakeholder considerations

In this section, we will discuss best practices and strategies for collaborating with other parties through the ecosystem and show how an understanding of circular market dynamics can enable and accelerate the adoption of "purpose-driven" practices across the value chain at affordable prices.

A crucial step toward transformation is an understanding of the critical role of external stakeholders. In the book *Sustainability Edge*, a nine-stakeholder framework is presented to aid a company in its sustainability transformation journey.[6] It clarifies the complex relationships between stakeholders and how they impact a firm's sustainable business practices (see Figure 7.2). The authors argue that sustainable business practices must consider the needs and interests of all stakeholders, including customers, employees, investors, suppliers, communities, governments, NGOs, future generations, and the environment. It is important to know when to engage with each stakeholder and in what capacity. In this chapter, we will expand the framework and adapt it for B2B firms in the context of pricing.

To maintain competitive advantage and make progress on specific initiatives, companies need to understand what is available, when to engage with each party, and when to go it alone.

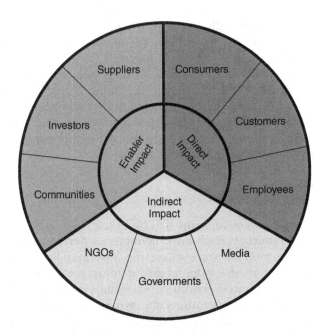

Figure 7.2 The nine-stakeholder model.

Source: Suhas Apte, and Jagdish N. Sheth, *Sustainability Edge: How to Drive Top-Line Growth with Triple-Bottom-Line Thinking* (Wharton Digital Press, 2016).

Our research has found that many collaboration opportunities are ignored by manufacturers. Even when manufacturers are aware of potential collaborators, they lack knowledge of, and awareness of best practices for, how and when to engage with ecosystem members and leverage the connection. It takes time and effort to negotiate agreements with retailers and other value chain providers and get their customers on board to support the initiative.

The landscape of the circular economy

The Ellen MacArthur Foundation's "butterfly diagram" (Figure 7.3) shows the stakeholder involvement in the circular economy, the processes that connect them, and the markets within the economy.[7] It illustrates the flow of materials in a circular economy with two cycles: technical and biological. The technological cycle involves reusing, repairing, remanufacturing, and recycling materials. The biological cycle involves returning biodegradable materials to the Earth.

Many of the players and markets in the circular economy slip under the radar: their influence ideally needs to be more evident to companies embarking on this journey. The markets behind these systems can remain invisible, but often significantly impact a firm's ability to participate fully in the ecosystem. The availability barriers facing the various players in each part of the value chain go from collection to use of recycled materials.

Each of the bubbles in Figure 7.3 brings in a cost/price component that can affect the efficiency of the supply chain. The maturity of these markets and therefore their ability to produce sufficient quantity and consistent quality varies significantly from industry to industry. An immature market may require significant investment in education and in building the ecosystem.

The position in the value chain

As we mentioned above, firms will find their own paths along the sustainability journey. Each firm encounters a particular set of barriers depending on its stage along the Sustainability Continuum and its position in the value chain; it must act according to its position and the context within which it finds itself. To begin with, a firm must assess its operations and products to identify where it fits in the circular value chain. It needs to identify its own internal drive and motivation to embark on the transformation. All of this requires a deep understanding of the product or service's lifecycle,

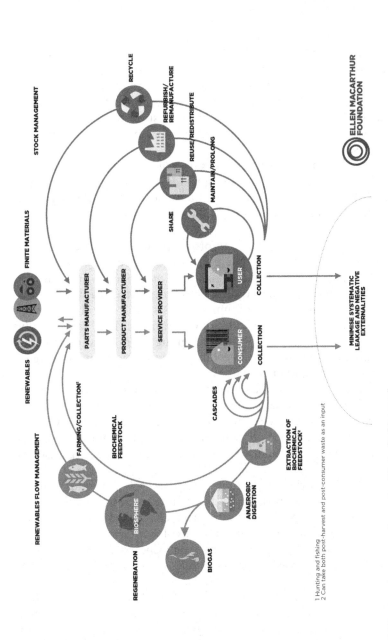

Figure 7.3 Circular economy systems: the "Butterfly Diagram".

Source: Ellen MacArthur Foundation, "The Butterfly Diagram: Visualising the Circular Economy." https://ellenmacarthurfoundation.org/circular-economy-diagram, accessed May 22, 2023.

Note: Drawing based on Braungart & McDonough, Cradle to Cradle (C2C).

from the sourcing of raw materials to the disposal or recycling of waste (see Figure 7.4).[8]

Once a firm has identified its place in the value chain, it can assess where it can add the most value. For example, a firm that operates in the *materials market* or as a primary raw materials manufacturer can add value by becoming an expert on industry standards on sustainability, reducing water usage and greenhouse emissions, and practicing social inclusivity and social development. This may involve sourcing raw materials from sustainable sources, reducing water use and greenhouse emissions during production, and promoting social development in the communities in which it operates.

Similarly, a firm that operates in the *components market* can add value by creating efficient designs for products and packaging materials, improving production efficiencies, and minimizing waste and energy use. This may involve designing products and packaging materials that are easy to recycle or reuse, using automation and digital technologies to improve production efficiency, and implementing strategies to minimize waste and energy use.

In the production of *packaging and materials*, a firm can add value by managing a light operational footprint, designing circularity into operations, and minimizing costs, waste, and energy use through efficient and productive operations. This may involve using renewable energy sources, designing operations to maximize the reuse and recycling of materials, and implementing strategies to minimize waste and energy use.

In the *distribution phase* of the circular value chain, firms can add value by minimizing handling, distance, energy use, carbon emissions, and costs. This may involve optimizing delivery routes and order volume management, using alternative modes of transportation, and implementing strategies to minimize energy use and carbon emissions.

Finally, firms that *collect waste and recycle* can add value by collecting pre- and post-consumer waste to be recycled, reusing materials in new packaging and products, and ensuring the high quality of raw materials. This may involve implementing effective collection and recycling systems, promoting consumer education on recycling and waste reduction, and working with suppliers to improve the quality of raw materials.

Overall, identifying where a firm falls in the *circular value chain* and *where it can add the most value requires a comprehensive assessment of its operations and products.* The feasibility of the project, the support of partners and collaborators, and the state of industry are all factors that can heavily influence the speed of progress. By taking a holistic approach to the circular economy, firms

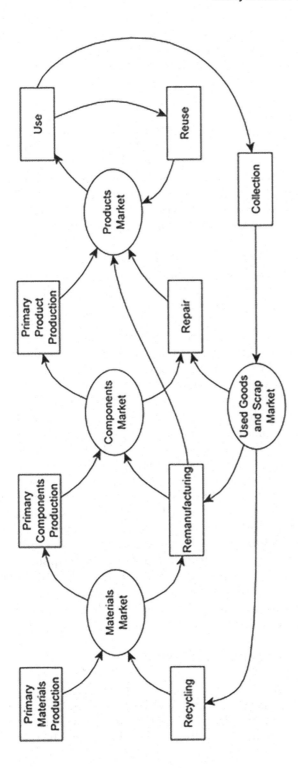

Figure 7.4 The markets in a circular economy.

Source: Thomas Siderius and Trevor Zink, *Markets and the Future of the Circular Economy, Circular Economy and Sustainability*, 2022.

can identify opportunities to reduce waste, minimize environmental impact, and create value for their stakeholders.

Various ecosystems are available to firms, from NGOs to governmental agencies and industry coalitions. Examples include the following:

- The *NextGen Cup Consortium*[9] is a multi-year, global consortium that aims to address single-use foodservice packaging waste by advancing the design, commercialization, and recovery of packaging alternatives. The Consortium works across the value chain – with brands, municipalities, material recovery facilities, and manufacturers – to provide viable market solutions that scale throughout the supply chain and bring value to recovery systems.
- The *Ellen MacArthur Foundation's* Circular Economy Network[10] brings together businesses, policymakers, innovators, universities, cities, philanthropic organizations, and thought leaders to build and scale a circular economy.

As a leading national force for improving recycling, *The Recycling Partnership*[11] puts private dollars to work in communities, works on the premises, and invests in a system to protect resources and empower sustainable action. This involves working with communities to improve the efficiency of their recycling programs, increasing public awareness about the importance of recycling, and providing funding to support recycling infrastructure. It works with multiple stakeholders, including local governments, businesses, waste management companies, and community organizations. The work may involve technical assistance to help these stakeholders implement recycling programs, offering funding to support the development of recycling infrastructure, or conducting research to identify opportunities for improving recycling rates. The Recycling Partnership also plays an essential role in advocating for policies that support the circular economy. This may involve working with lawmakers to develop legislation that promotes recycling and waste reduction or advocating for policies that support the development of recycling infrastructure.

Best practices for moving forward

Finding your purpose

If your organization is at the initial stage of the Sustainability Continuum, it might struggle to find the incentive to move to the next stage, especially if it is doing well. Change will be disruptive, and decision-makers must be convinced that the price of inaction (i.e., maintaining the status quo) exceeds the cost of change.

Consultancy firm BrightHouse,[12] which started in Atlanta, GA, and was later acquired by Boston Consulting Group (BCG), helps its clients embark on the "Purpose" journey. It can actually take a long time for a company to identify the core belief that drove the initial founders to launch their product or service. BrightHouse consultants go to great lengths to get to that real reason. The founders of the company that produced the Goldfish snack (now owned by Campbell Soup Company), as it turned out, believed in putting a smile on children's faces; if you look at the ingredient list today, you will see the first ingredient in the list is "smiles." After getting into a lot of trouble with the controversy around their Dove and Axe campaigns, Unilever sought to change internally and become an authentic organization. Whether or not the firm can claim to be part of a circularity ecosystem, understanding its contribution to the value chain and authentically delivering that value requires a sophistication many firms still lack. Reconnecting with your organization's original mission and goals is an essential part of a complete transformation. This is an activity that can be part of the "Offense" rather than the "Defense" positioning.

Once your company has zoned in on where it can add the most impact, the next challenge along the journey concerns availability and feasibility. WestRock is one of the largest paper and packaging companies[13] and produces fiber-based packaging using an operating model that is inherently circular. Its source material – fiber from sustainably harvested trees – is a renewable resource. It invests heavily in R&D and design to create consumer-preferred, highly recyclable packaging. Furthermore, its manufacturing processes (papermaking and packaging) are based on circularity: it uses outputs from papermaking to generate power and steam; it recycles and reuses water in its facilities; and large quantities of recycled paper go into producing new paper. WestRock also recovers paper- and fiber-based packaging post-use, operating 18 recycling facilities across the U.S., where it gathers the recyclables for use in its papermaking. WestRock is an example of a company with many roles across the circular economy: supplier, producer, recycler, and reuser.

Many firms are being forced to act because of pressure from their customers and employees. Retailers are drawing up sustainability programs, setting goals, and communicating them to their consumers. To fulfill these goals, they are reaching out to their suppliers and the markets supporting the chain. However, in B2B companies, the transition to environmentally sustainable product design could be faster, and a full-scale transformation can take years.

For example, as we saw above, Walmart has committed to ESG and requires suppliers such as its Consumer Products Group (CPG) manufacturing firms to follow suit. However, this creates upstream issues. For example, if the giant U.S. food manufacturer General Mills wants sustainably sourced ingredients and packaging, it will reach out to the farmers and the paper manufacturers. Now the cereal paper box manufacturer (for example) will, in turn, need to change its manufacturing processes. That company will incur costs related to R&D, new manufacturing processes, sourcing of recycled materials, etc. Two options are possible here: (1) General Mills pays the paper company a higher price and then passes the costs to its consumers via a price premium. In this case, the consumer pays for having an environmentally friendly cereal box. Not all consumers are willing to pay this green premium, which slows down demand and holds back the adoption of environmentally friendly products. (2) Collaborate with industry, government, and across the value chain to share/identify alternative revenue streams. Some of these ideas are discussed later in this chapter.

Currently, there is much discussion about "who pays" and how the additional costs could be shared among the different players: consumers, manufacturers, and the supply chain ecosystems. In addition, many B2B firms need help in deciding when to invest in "purpose-driven" activities and how to manage some of the resulting costs. Industry coalitions and strategic agreements are essential in the early stages to share costs, knowledge, and resources in order to redesign, innovate, and think creatively about economically sound and purpose-driven alternatives. Joint investments in technology and social development may be necessary for markets to move forward. Below, we explore some best practices that may provide some economically justifiable strategies.

Joint investments

In 2020, Unilever launched its "Partner with Purpose" program to jointly innovate and increase both transparency and growth.[14] Through this program, the company has created an ecosystem of providers that collaborate in a mission to develop and create new products better aligned with "purpose." For example, in partnership with Evonik, Unilever developed rhamnolipids, chemicals that are safe and can be used in commercial cleaning products. Three firms came together, including Viridor, a U.K. waste management company, to develop plastic packaging with a detectable black pigment, which enables recycling plant scanners to sort it for recycling. It's now used on the TRESemmé and Lynx brands.

The Closed Loop Leadership Fund (of Closed Loop Partners) is Unilever's private equity group. The fund, which handled $15 million of Unilever's funds in 2021, invests in companies that improve recycling capabilities and contribute to keeping materials in the circular economy.[15] Coca-Cola has developed similar partnerships with its ecosystem of suppliers to create an enabling environment for clean water and recycled packaging as well as encouraging a socially inclusive culture.

Blended finance is another strategy used for ESG-related investments. It refers to the use of a combination of public and private sector funds, resources, and expertise to finance projects and investments that promote sustainable and responsible business practices. The goal of blended finance for ESG is to mobilize additional capital for initiatives that address environmental, social, and governance challenges, such as climate change, poverty alleviation, gender equality, and ethical corporate governance. The return expectations are lower and, hence, you can structure a deal with societal and environmental goals.

Strategic partnerships: manage the price relationships with knowledge-sharing

Strategic partnerships are as old as business itself and can provide win–win solutions for the parties involved. The success of such partnerships hinges on inter-organizational trust and knowledge sharing in order to allocate resources and facilitate coordination, creativity, and integration. Knowledge sharing helps firms compete effectively and deliver value-added products. Knowledge can drive effective solutions and lead to joint goals and common strategies.

Coca-Cola routinely partners with many of the retailers that sell its products, including fast-food restaurants. In fact, the drinks giant has whole teams dedicated to helping its retail customers succeed and improve overall sales. By sharing knowledge and best practices, they help organize processes and streamline products and prices – for example, by setting menus to match prices, which, in turn, boost the sales of Coca-Cola products.

Knowledge sharing of this kind can be a real boon for a company moving forward with environmentally sustainable products and looking to source raw materials and formulate, design, package, and price them. A retailer's expertise and experience with other suppliers can be invaluable to a company that wants to scale its environmentally sustainable products. Such partnerships can constitute a competitive edge. Knowledge sharing is leverage: in developing a trusting inter-organizational relationship, the long-term viability of circularity resources can be ensured, and innovative ways can be found to solve problems.

Sharing value, not price

As discussed, it is often the retailers that push manufacturers toward more sustainable processes. The usual expectation, however, is to swallow the increased costs. If that's the case, suppliers need to find other areas on which to negotiate to compensate for their reduced margins. There are some creative ways to enable a manufacturer to begin the sustainability journey when price is not on the table. Instead of negotiating on price, how about negotiating on *value*? In 2022, after 40-year record inflation, large retailers such as Walmart were pushing back on product manufacturers' price increases. So, those product companies must instead look more broadly at value, which involves improving efficiencies, reducing costs, and increasing sales volume. Below are some examples:

- **Favorable shelf space.** It is no secret that favorable shelf space – e.g., at the corners of the category aisle or at eye level – can significantly impact sales. When it is difficult to negotiate on price, negotiate on premium visibility. Prominent positioning of a product can affect brand perception and awareness and improve a customer's propensity to purchase. It's estimated that favorable shelf positioning can provide a revenue lift of over 15%.[16]
- **In-store promotions.** Co-branding can boost your brand and sales. In an example from Mexico, Newell Brands' "Mr. Coffee" coffee maker was perceived as a high-end elite-branded appliance. Newell wanted to rebrand the product image to appeal to the higher end of the growing middle class. Co-branding (as well as offering free, locally produced coffee with purchases) was seen as an effective strategy. Trade promotions can also help foreground a product and communicate its societal impact.
- **Be a client reference.** Another great way to get value from retailers is to offer to be the client reference or to co-present at user conferences. Becoming a premium partner can have benefits for both parties. Take the case of an ice cream manufacturer that supplies locally produced ice cream to Whole Foods Market, the U.S. supermarket giant. Although the manufacturer only makes a tiny margin by selling to Whole Foods, its partnership with the company has led to the firm doing more business elsewhere and has endowed it with increased credibility.
- **Promote manufacturing at industry conferences.** Showcasing win–win partnerships can also help the firm build recognition in the industry, share best practices, and grow the business.

- **Volume orders.** Volume orders from a retailer can reduce inventory carrying costs and also lower shipping costs, indirectly improving profitability. For example, shipments could be sent quarterly rather than monthly.
- **Favorable contractual/payment terms.** Manufacturers often offer retailers long payment terms –maybe up to 180 days – as an enticement. But this has the downside of tying up working capital and incurs the opportunity cost of not having the funds for up to six months. Better payment terms mean a quicker turnout of working cash flow, which can also reduce borrowing costs.
- **Price guarantees.** Another area for negotiation: ask retailers to guarantee a price range. A retailer is usually at liberty to sell a manufacturer's product at whatever price it chooses. However, lowering the price below a certain level can impact brand image. On the other hand, failing to roll out price promotions can inhibit sales. Manufacturers would often appreciate more control in this area. Apple is one of the few firms that manages to ensure a consistent and harmonized price across all countries by incentivizing retailers to adhere to the desired price. This has positively impacted Apple's brand image and profitability.
- **Data-sharing agreements.** This is best exemplified by the relationship between consumer goods multinational Procter & Gamble (P&G) and Walmart. The firms share data on ordering and inventory, thanks to Walmart's automated reordering system.[17] This results in reduced inefficiencies and a lowering of costs for P&G. Data sharing helps the firm improve its analytics capability, predictive capacity, and supply chain efficiency. It is a win–win as it also gives access to a wealth of highly useful data to the retailer about the thousands of products it stocks.

Key takeaways

In addition to aligning internal systems and processes, firms must also align with suppliers, customers, and the various stakeholders involved in the product and service.

- Many markets in the business-to-business (B2B) part of the value chain are invisible but nonetheless have a significant influence on prices.
- Potential collaborators may be able to help break through the motivation, knowledge, availability, and affordability barriers. Partnering with key stakeholders in the value chain – understanding their motivation and barriers – will be vital in getting ecosystems to work together towards pro-social goals.

- It may not always be possible to get a price premium for environmentally friendly products. Manufacturers need to be strategic to cover additional costs and explore other ways to share value created. The circular economy needs suppliers to be creative in how they collaborate across the value chain, with joint investment and strategic partnerships sharing knowledge and value.

Notes

1 "Walmart Announces New Plastic Packaging Waste Reduction Commitments." Walmart, February 27, 2019. https://corporate.walmart.com/news/2019/02/26/walmart-announces-new-plastic-packaging-waste-reduction-commitments
2 "Responsible Consumption and Production. Goal 12: Ensure Sustainable Consumption and Production Patterns." LyondellBasell, April 2021. https://www.lyondellbasell.com/en/sustainability/un-sustainable-development-goals/responsible-consumption-and-production
3 Karen Laird, "SABIC Commits to Production of 1 Million Metric Tons of Circular Materials by 2030." Sustainable Plastics, January 20, 2023. https://www.sustainableplastics.com/news/sabic-commits-production-1million-tonnes-circular-materials-2030
4 "Dow Commits to Accelerating the Circular Ecosystem by Transforming Waste and Alternative Feedstock to Deliver 3 Million Metric Tons per Year of Circular and Renewable Solutions by 2030." Dow Inc., press release, October 17, 2022. https://corporate.dow.com/en-us/news/press-releases/dow-commits-to-accelerating-the-circular-ecosystem-by-transformi.html
5 Sarah Hadley, "Recycled PET Market: Supply and Demand Market Issues," Plastic Collective, September 7, 2022. https://www.plasticcollective.co/recycled-pet-market-supply-demand-market-issues
6 Suhas Apte and Jagdish N. Sheth, Sustainability Edge: How to Drive Top-Line Growth with Triple-Bottom-Line Thinking (Wharton Digital Press, 2016).
7 Ellen MacArthur Foundation, "The Butterfly Diagram: Visualising the Circular Economy." https://ellenmacarthurfoundation.org/circular-economy-diagram
8 Thomas Siderius and Trevor Zink, "Markets and the Future of the Circular Economy." Circular Economy and Sustainability, August 24, 2022. https://doi.org/10.1007/s43615-022-00196-4
9 "The NextGen Consortium: Accelerating the Circular Future of Foodservice Packaging," Closed Loop Partners, March 14, 2023. https://www.closedlooppartners.com/nextgen
10 Ellen MacArthur Foundation, "The World's Leading Circular Economy Network." https://ellenmacarthurfoundation.org/network/overview
11 "The Recycling Partnership Releases Strategy for Improving U.S. Recycling." The Recycling Partnership, November 15, 2022. https://recyclingpartnership.org/the-recycling-partnership-releases-strategy-for-improving-u-s-recycling

12 https://bcgbrighthouse.com

13 https://www.westrock.com

14 Unilever, "Partner with Purpose." https://www.unilever.com/suppliers/partner-with-purpose

15 Megan Smalley, "Unilever Invests $15M in Closed Loop Partners' Leadership Fund." *Recycling Today*, March 16, 2021. https://www.recyclingtoday.com/news/unilever-invests-15-million-closed-loop-leadership-fund-recycle-plastic

16 Sylvester da Cunha, "The Science behind Shelf Placement." *The Economic Times*, January 20, 2010. https://economictimes.indiatimes.com/the-science-behind-shelf-placement/articleshow/5478934.cms

17 Matt Waller, "How Sharing Data Drives Supply Chain Innovation." *IndustryWeek*, August 12, 2013. https://www.industryweek.com/supply-chain/supplier-relationships/article/21960963/how-sharing-data-drives-supply-chain-innovation

8 Future implications

The future depends on what you do today.

Mahatma Gandhi

In the development process, product design and raw materials significantly influence cost implications and, hence, the price floor. Smarter innovation at this stage is a route to reducing costs and, therefore, prices. How customers use the product, how often they buy and reuse it, both frequency and quantity, influence pricing decisions. It's quite straightforward: society benefits when innovation results in the development of new technology that is better for society and available at affordable prices. However, innovation can come in product, manufacturing process or in the after sales process. In this chapter we discuss opportunites for the future in light of pricing.

Accelerate product innovation for products that are better for planet and people

Innovation in product development and raw materials can drive the future to reduce costs and, hence, reduce prices to make products more accessible to broader populations is the center of this strategy. Companies like Beyond Meat and Impossible Foods were initially hailed as game-changers that would disrupt the global meat industry with their plant-based meat substitutes. This was mainly due to their potential to save extraordinary carbon emissions by reducing meat consumption. Ultimately, however, these firms have faced challenges and limitations in achieving widespread adoption. The factors contributing to this are complex and include issues around taste, cost, distribution, and cultural attitudes toward meat consumption. Despite these obstacles, the meat-alternative market is still growing and evolving and has the potential to impact the future of the food industry. The emergence of this product has started to relieve the burden of responsibility that beef production has borne in feeding the planet and the associated costs. And more affordable pricing will increase take-up and penetration of the product distribution and consumption globally.

DOI: 10.4324/9781032659008-10

Promoting reuse

Fast fashion has harmed the planet in several ways. The annual carbon emissions from the fashion industry are now greater than the combined emissions from all international flights and maritime shipping. If the industry continues on its current path, greenhouse emissions are predicted to increase by 50% within the next decade. Fast-fashion companies get their clothes to market rapidly, leading to a surplus of items that quickly become outdated and discarded. This has led to a significant increase in textile waste, with many clothes ending up in landfills or incinerators. Textile production requires large amounts of water, and the chemicals used in the dyeing and finishing processes can pollute local waterways and ecosystems. The energy-intensive production process and global transportation are the sources of most of the greenhouse gases for which the industry is responsible. And, because of the rapidly advertised cycle of trends to which the fast-fashion industry caters, it promotes a culture of *overconsumption* and *constant purchasing*, in which consumers are encouraged to buy new items frequently rather than investing in high-quality items that will last longer. In response to these concerns, many fashion houses are looking for alternatives.

Patagonia is a company taking steps to reduce its environmental impact. With its "Worn Wear" program, it encourages customers to repair and reuse their Patagonia clothing rather than buy new items, thereby reducing textile waste. Patagonia offers free repairs for all its clothing items, as well as a trade-in program in which customers can receive credit toward new items by sending in their used Patagonia clothing. The company also sells used items on its website, further promoting the idea of reusing clothing rather than constantly buying new things. Similarly, H&M uses more sustainable materials and has launched a garment recycling program. Nike has been increasing the amount of recycled materials in its products. A major focus has been recycled polyester from discarded plastic bottles and other sources. For instance, Nike's "Reuse-A-Shoe" program collects old athletic shoes and grinds them down to create material for new products. These programs add new costs and hence require new business models. The prospect of reduced revenue has to be factored in if customers buy fewer new shoes and clothes. This will result in developing new pricing models geared towards allowing for reuse and resale or having third-party ownership structures.

Pricing and Artificial Intelligence

Recent advancements in Artificial Intelligence (AI), spearheaded by technology giants such as Google, Apple, and Amazon, have led to remarkable progress and innovation. This technological evolution can transform the interactions between businesses and consumers, improving customer experiences, personalized prices, and increased sales. Using analytical prowess to process vast data sets it enables a deeper understanding of customer behaviors. This evolution includes adopting pricing AI strategies, such as machine learning, which identifies significant patterns in consumer spending.

- These advanced techniques move beyond traditional, rigid pricing models, accommodating variations in customer price sensitivity. For instance, if a customer less concerned about prices tends not to compare prices before buying, machine learning algorithms can detect this pattern. This insight allows businesses to tailor pricing strategies more effectively, ensuring that different customer segments are charged optimally based on their observed willingness to pay.
- In e-commerce, AI will play a pivotal role, particularly in offering *personalized recommendations* through machine learning algorithms. These algorithms analyze customer data like browsing history and purchase habits, tailoring product suggestions accordingly. Accenture's research reveals that 91% of consumers prefer brands that provide personalized experiences. Such customization enhances customer engagement, sales, and loyalty. AI powers different types of recommendation engines: collaborative filtering (using user–item interactions), content-based filtering (analyzing item features), and hybrid approaches (combining both methods). Major e-commerce entities like Amazon, Netflix, and Stitch Fix have leveraged these technologies, significantly boosting sales and customer engagement. Amazon utilizes collaborative filtering to drive 35% of its sales through personalized suggestions, while Netflix's hybrid system accounts for 80% of content viewed. Stitch Fix combines machine learning with human stylists for tailored clothing recommendations.
- AI algorithms in *dynamic pricing* consider customer attributes, market trends, seasonality, and inventory management. This strategy enhances sales, profit margins, and customer satisfaction. Companies like Uber, and airlines, and online retailers like Amazon and Walmart, have successfully implemented dynamic pricing, achieving substantial market benefits. Integrating AI in e-commerce optimization, encompassing personalized recommendations and dynamic pricing, will dramatically influence pricing. Personalized pricing – pricing for each individual

person – and customized discounts are ways that AI pricing models can evolve.

However, the technology may exploit the willingness to pay beyond what the creators envisioned. For example, research conducted by Firasta-Vastani and Monroe, 2019[1] in the *Journal of Services Marketing* demonstrates that women are more price-sensitive and have smaller price acceptance bands than men. Would an AI algorithm, left unchecked, charge men more for household supplies than women? How would race, socioeconomic status, and geographic differences play into personalized pricing? Diversity, equity, and inclusion (DEI) are key areas for companies to ensure all customers are treated fairly.

Ubiquitous use of AI in pricing can potentially develop racial bias, predatory pricing behaviors, and unethical pricing practices. An HBR article, "AI Can Help Address Inequity – If Companies Earn Users' Trust,"[2] demonstrated the inadvertent dangers of AI. For example, Airbnb's pricing algorithm aimed to reduce income disparities between Black and White hosts. While it successfully decreased this gap by 71.3% among those who used it, Black hosts were 41% less likely to adopt the tool, inadvertently exacerbating the income disparity in many cases. Black hosts see higher price elasticity on their properties, and, by using the algorithm, they can reduce prices to increase occupancy and, hence, revenue. This highlights the necessity for companies to anticipate how their algorithms will be received and devise strategies that foster trust, particularly among intended users like Black hosts. Two critical takeaways emerge: the importance of understanding an algorithm's perception and the need for a tailored approach to cultivate trust and understanding of use.

Key takeaways

In conclusion, product, process, and technological innovation in business represents a transformative era of growth and competitive edge for businesses. As technologies evolve, the future of e-commerce optimization looks promising, offering sophisticated tools to navigate the dynamic landscape. Adopting these innovations and addressing forthcoming challenges will enable businesses to thrive in this ever-changing domain. However, companies can be aware of and train the new innovations and technologies with the ethos of purpose-driven pricing so that innovation can continue to exhibit the firm's core values.

Notes

1 S.F. Vastani and K.B. Monroe, "Role of Customer Attributes on Absolute Price Thresholds." *Journal of Services Marketing* 33(5) (2019): 589–601.
2 Shunyuan Zhang, Kannan Srinivasan, Param Singh, and Nitin Mehta. "AI Can Help Address Inequity – If Companies Earn Users' Trust." *Harvard Business Review*, Digital Articles, September 17, 2021.

Part III

Case studies

9 Case studies: The seven tactics

There are a thousand ways to kneel and kiss the ground.

Rumi

Many firms still view "purpose" and "profit" as an either/or decision, at least in the short term. In this book, we've discussed both short- and long-term pro-social pricing strategies for firms to manage this dilemma. In this section, we summarize some of these ideas, along with some new case studies and tactics. Seven strategies are presented in all, including real-world cases and examples, and these are: unbundling, bundling, resizing, the role of free, new monetization models, cost engineering, and green premium. Hopefully, these concepts can effectively help demonstrate how pricing strategies can be used to balance business and societal objectives. Should we invest in purpose-led efforts, increasing our costs, or drag our feet, postponing this expense until it becomes a real problem? Today, we are seeing more and more examples of companies incorporating social good into their business without forsaking financial goals.

Firms of Endearment is a book by Raj Sisodia, Jagdish Sheth, and David Wolfe which explains why doing good not only benefits society, but can also confer a strong competitive advantage. The authors ask us to consider not just "share of wallet" but also "share of heart." Doing the right thing is ultimately better for the company, and doing good for a customer roughly equates to doing good for the planet or society. In fact, these aims frequently go hand in hand, with profits, purpose, and price all aligned.[1] Companies that have a one-dimensional view of profits will become dinosaurs.

Seven pricing tactics to manage transitions and accelerate transformations

1. Unbundling

One way to reduce an offer's price is to unbundle it. Unbundling is the practice of breaking down a product or service into its individual

DOI: 10.4324/9781032659008-12

components or features. This strategy often saves customers money by allowing them to pay only for the specific elements they want.

Costs directly impact pricing decisions, and whether or not you advocate cost-based pricing, they form a price floor. A price floor is the lowest price at which a firm should sell a product and is typically only the marginal cost of the product or service. Maximizing cost efficiencies means lower price floors and, as a result, the flexibility to charge lower prices and aim for higher market shares. Cost savings from unbundling benefit customers by allowing lower prices, but they may also minimize a company's costs from waste and misuse of products and services that are not needed. An unbundling strategy can be observed in various industries, such as telecommunications, media, and software. Here are a few examples:

- In the past, telecommunications companies offered bundled packages which includes a landline phone service, internet access, and cable TV. The downside of this was that customers were forced to pay for a broad range of channels, even if they only wanted to watch a few. However, with the rise of streaming services and internet-based communication, many providers are unbundling their content and subscriptions, offering separate packages for each service, essentially allowing customers to build their own plans and pay only for what they require.
- Software companies, rather than selling complete software suites, may offer individual applications or modules separately. Customers can then select the necessary components, thus avoiding paying for unnecessary features.
- Carriers have used the strategy, too. Instead of offering a comprehensive package including checked baggage, in-flight meals, and seat selection, airlines are charging separately for these services. Passengers can decide whether to pay extra for additional services or to opt for a basic fare with no extras.

Unbundling Apple

When companies offer unbundled products or services, they streamline their operations, and the positive impact is felt both ways: firms spend no more than they need, and customers avoid paying for things they won't use. Similarly, firms that offer services like extended payment terms, service guarantees, or training can unbundle these, too, providing goods at the same or even lower prices.

In October 2020, with the launch of the iPhone 12 series, Apple announced its decision to stop shipping chargers and earphones with its iPhones.[2] The company's stated reason was to reduce its carbon footprint and address environmental concerns. With this move, packaging size was reduced, thus reducing the number of shipments required and, therefore, the associated carbon emissions. Apple hopes to encourage its customers to use their existing accessories (from previous models) rather than purchase new ones, which should help reduce electronic waste.

The decision initially met with criticism from customers, who felt they should receive all the necessary accessories, but environmental advocates applauded Apple's efforts to promote more sustainable practices within the tech industry. Up to March 2022, this move has saved Apple $6.5 billion.[3] Apple can ship more phones simultaneously by stacking more boxes on a pallet. Consequently, smaller box sizes could cut Apple's annual carbon emissions by 2 million metric tons, akin to removing 500,000 cars from the roads, according to the company.

Unbundling the MBA

A Deloitte study has demonstrated how both digital and non-digital offerings can be unbundled.[4] One of the examples was corporate education, specifically the MBA program.

Corporate education is undergoing significant changes as companies adapt to remain viable. Two-year MBA programs are threatened by other options, such as on-the-job management training and other personal/business development programs, normally offered by corporations and third-party providers. Traditional MBA programs are notoriously expensive due to costs associated with physical infrastructure, the remuneration of "name" professors, and brand reputation. At the same time, students are faced with a significant time commitment and a potential loss of earnings during their time in the program. Business schools have introduced accelerated, part-time, and low-residency options, but the core components of lectures, practice, community, networking, accreditation, and career placement often remain confined to physical campuses.

Non-traditional education providers have capitalized on the shift to virtual content distribution, focusing on non-traditional settings like corporate learning centers. Here, the cost of management training is greatly reduced, as the expertise required is less formal and can be offered by practitioners using virtual resources. Stand-alone corporate learning centers have multiplied 10x from 2005.

These new offerings have put pressure on traditional MBA programs, as witnessed by declining application numbers for full-time two-year programs. This trend has caught the attention of educators and institutions, including prestigious ones like Harvard Business

School. Many higher-education institutions are unbundling their services, too, offering components of traditional business degree programs in more customizable, affordable, or on-demand formats. Massive Open Online Course (MOOC) platforms provide lectures, while specialized institutions and incubators offer training in entrepreneurship and specific sectors and also provide access to networks for guidance, funding, and career opportunities.[5]

By prioritizing MOOCs and corporate education, universities may divert demand from their longer, high-margin two-year programs, potentially leading to a lasting shift in customer mindset. While established brands may slow down the unbundling effect, customer expectations and educational technology models are evolving at a rapid rate and will continue to shape the higher-education landscape.

2. Bundling

Bundling strategies vary, but their ultimate outcome is to improve companies' sustainability and reduce prices, especially when they combine products or services in a way that encourages eco-friendly practices and offers cost-effective solutions to customers. The concept can be widely observed, from online streaming services to products on grocery store shelves. It relies on consumers' willingness to buy a bundle because they perceive the savings as a gain rather than focusing on the individual cost of each item. Here are some examples of how bundling can be effective in rolling out and encouraging the adoption of environmentally friendly products.

Other bundling options are member pricing, volume discounts, better rates, or unique event invitations to reward customers who are willing to buy "purpose-driven" products. This would be particularly important for products that actually fare worse with regard to performance and functionality in comparison with conventional counterparts. In such a case, at least one of the products in the bundle needs to be price-sensitive so that its price reduction will encourage customers to buy the whole bundle.

- Companies in the renewable energy sector can bundle solar panels with other energy storage solutions, like batteries, offering customers a means of not just generating solar power but also storing the excess for use during non-sunny periods. By reducing the overall cost of purchasing solar panels and batteries separately, this strategy also encourages environmentally friendly behavior.
- Some fashion companies, such as H&M, have created capsule collections consisting of sustainably produced clothing items, often made of organic cotton or recycled fibers designed to be

mixed and matched. By bundling a few essential pieces to create multiple outfits, companies promote more conscious consumption and reduce the number of items in customers' wardrobes. And, of course, the total price of the capsule bundle is lower than if a customer bought each item individually.

• Some travel companies are creating sustainable travel packages, which include eco-friendly accommodation options, carbon-offset flight credits, and eco-tourism activities. Bundling these elements saves customers money and makes it easy for them to choose more environmentally friendly options.

• Online retailers provide free shipping versus charging for shipping separately is another exanple of bundling.

Bundling Amazon packages

Amazon's sustainability initiative is aimed at achieving "Shipment Zero," an ultimate goal of making all Amazon shipments net zero carbon, with an interim target of 50% of all shipments net zero by 2030. On "Amazon Day," if a customer places multiple orders within a short period, and the items can be shipped from the same fulfillment center or nearby locations, Amazon will bundle the items into a single shipment. This reduces shipping costs and delivery time, with the added benefit of not bombarding customers with numerous packages. Amazon's Frustration-Free Packaging program aims to reduce the amount of packaging materials while making the packages easier to open. Amazon Prime members can even choose an Amazon Day for their deliveries. Plus, customers can get the incentive of a small discount to encourage them to bundle their deliveries.

3. Reducing size

In Chapter 4, on behavioral pricing, we discussed the idea of "shrinkflation." When companies reduce the size of the package just within the perceptual threshold but hold the price constant, they are effectively increasing the price per unit. And, since many customers do not notice small changes in package size, companies can increase prices without a loss in demand.

Shrinkflation to manage circular product availability

In 2023, Coca-Cola launched a new bottle made with 100% recycled plastic, which held 13.2 oz (374 g), approximately 21% less than its regular 16.9 oz bottles (479 g). The price for both sizes, however, was the same: $1.59. The smaller bottle has benefits: there is less packaging, and less raw material goes into making the bottle, thus lowering manufacturing costs. In addition, customers end up drinking less of a product that has a reputation for contributing to obesity. Coca-Cola's reduced costs give the company room to accommodate the increased cost of making the bottles out of 100% recycled material. From many perspectives, it's a beneficial change.[6]

Reducing size for health benefits

Larger portion sizes and increased food consumption contribute to issues such as overweight and obesity, as well as heightened food waste. Furthermore, the presence of larger portions can distort individuals' perceptions of what constitutes an "appropriate" serving size. This phenomenon, often called the 'portion size effect,' persists even when people are consistently exposed to larger portions for extended periods, prompting calls for portion size reductions.

Analyzing data from three national surveys encompassing over 60,000 Americans, researchers at the University of North Carolina at Chapel Hill have discerned a trend of escalating serving sizes from 1977 to 1996. This phenomenon extends beyond fast-food establishments and encompasses other restaurants as well as home-cooked meals. According to the study's authors, Samara Joy Nielsen and Barry M. Popkin, during these two decades, food portion sizes increased both within and outside the home across all categories except pizza, with the magnitude of these increases being substantial.

- Hamburgers have expanded by 23%.
- A typical serving of Mexican food has increased by 27%.
- Soft drinks have seen a notable 52% size augmentation.
- Snack items, spanning potato chips, pretzels, and crackers, have surged in size by a considerable 60%.

The researchers also noted that the prevalence of adult obesity in the United States has surged from 14.5% in 1971 to 30.9% in 1999. Reducing food portion sizes could potentially reset people's expectations of what constitutes a normal serving size, potentially leading to the selection of smaller portions in the future. Reduced portion size, yet keeping prices constant, will enable restaurants to source healthier, more sustainable food alternatives and reduce waste.

Alleviate poverty

In Chapter 1, we discussed C.K. Prahalad's book *The Fortune at the Bottom of the Pyramid*[7] which encourages multinationals to make products for the lower socio-economic strata as a way to reduce poverty and improve profits. The book describes the "4 A's" to address the challenges and opportunities of serving the economically disadvantaged population at the base of the economic pyramid.

- Businesses must create *awareness* about their products and services among their target customers. This means effective marketing campaigns communicating benefits and unique selling propositions. An understanding of target customers' needs and preferences is vital, so market research is needed to identify the key drivers of customer behavior, such as demographics, psychographics, and purchasing patterns.
- *Availability* The ease with which customers can find your products or services. This is critical because customers are more likely to buy from companies that make their products and services easily accessible, i.e., available in the right places at the correct times via online marketplaces, physical retail stores, or distribution channels.
- *Acceptability* The likelihood that customers will purchase it again; in other words, the determining factor in the level of loyalty and repeat business that a company can expect. Repurchase intent is the reward for companies that deliver high-quality products and services, provide excellent customer service, and build solid customer relationships.
- *Affordability* The ability to price at a level that works for your target customers. There is a balance to be found between pricing and profitability, along with the smart use of discounts and promotions to attract price-sensitive customers.

To extend consumer accessibility to their products, companies often develop streamlined variants (Chakravarthy & Coughlan, 2012)[8] of their offerings, positioned as more budget-friendly options for the base of the economic pyramid. This approach empowers consumers with increased purchasing capacity, enabling them to acquire other necessary products. Many countries are still cash economies, and having products available in *smaller sizes* improves the ability to buy high-quality products that last longer. These stripped-down alternatives, while different and more affordable than their original counterparts, still provide substantial value, maintain quality, and retain functionality, all while remaining accessible to cost-conscious consumers.

Price packs are sales promotions marked on the package such as buy one get one free, 10% off, etc. Additionally, companies offer price packs at significantly reduced rates for consumers at the base of the economic pyramid. Price packs not only offer affordability to this demographic but also provide consumers with greater product quantities, eliminating concerns about future purchases. Notable examples of price packs include Nestlé's $0.30 single-serve dry milk sachets and Pepsodent Triple Clean toothbrushes, priced at $0.20. These economically-priced items enable consumers at the base of the pyramid to acquire products that enhance their quality of life.

In 2009, Godrej Appliances introduced the "Chotukool," an unsucessful example of an innovative portable refrigerator designed for the rural Indian market, where a significant portion of food is lost due to spoilage. By incorporating solid-state cooling technology and eliminating the need for a traditional compressor, the company drastically reduced power consumption to a mere 62 watts and halved the price of an entry-level refrigerator, making it accessible at just $69. This product operates on a battery, weighs less than 10 pounds, and effectively preserves food freshness at temperatures ranging from 40 to 60 degrees Fahrenheit. Today, multiple versions of the Chotukool are manufactured and distributed through retail channels, reaching consumers across various socioeconomic strata. However inspite the efforts the products has limited distribution as the price point is still high for the target market, and cheaper alertatives were already present. Pricing needs to be diruptive to be successful in bottom of the pyramid markets.

4. The role of "free"

In Chapter 5, on the role of government, we argued for charging a nominal price rather than giving something away for free. Setting a price, however nominal, affects consumption levels and can result in less waste and more reuse. A study in Uganda, which compared the use of free mosquito nets against those that had been paid for, found that the paid-for nets were being used more consistently and more effectively than the free ones.[9] This not only results in cost savings from using fewer nets, but also reduces financial donations needed to run the program, and results in better health outcomes for the locals. A win–win–win solution!

Parking

Take the example of free parking and the burden it places on society. According to UCLA professor Donald Shoup, much of the problem associated with America's car culture can be directly attributed to irrational attitudes toward parking. He argues that the oversupply of free parking – which accounts for an estimated 99% of parking in the U.S. – is a significant public subsidy that artificially lowers the cost of driving and skews travel choices.[10] It's a situation that mirrors the "Tragedy of the Commons" seen in the overuse of unowned resources.

Zoning requirements, especially ones that mandate excessive off-street parking and fail to charge reasonable prices for curb parking, have negative consequences such as increased air pollution, higher oil consumption, traffic congestion, and urban sprawl. Additionally, the cost of housing, goods, and services all increase as a result of parking requirements. In his book,[11] Shoup points to the levels of air pollution that are caused by cars circling around to look for free parking. If parking prices were adjusted, demand might shift to other times of the day, or alternative travel choices might even be the outcome. Having reviewed 16 American and European studies conducted between 1927 and 2001, he concluded that cars searching for free parking contribute to over 8% of total traffic.

Urban planners factor in a certain number of parking spaces for each development. This requirement both increases the cost of housing and reduces its availability – and this impact is not restricted to just low-income housing. According to a study conducted in San Francisco, mandates for off-street parking resulted in an average increase of $47,000 in housing prices and an increase of $67,000–76,000 for the minimum annual household income necessary to purchase a home. Shoup asserts that parking charges would reduce this unwanted effect on housing, pollution, and traffic and that the increased parking revenue could be used to offset other governmental charges.

5. Changing the monetization model

Value-based pricing models for healthcare

In recent years, pay-for-performance (P4P) and value-based healthcare compensation models are approaches that are becoming popular. This type of pricing model incentivizes healthcare providers based on the quality and efficiency of care they deliver rather than simply the volume of services provided. In P4P, providers are rewarded for meeting specific performance benchmarks, with bonuses or penalties tied to outcomes and adherence to clinical guidelines. Value-based models, on the other hand, encompass a broader range of components, including quality metrics, cost control, shared savings, and risk sharing, aiming to improve healthcare value by aligning incentives with both quality and cost-effectiveness. These models promote improved quality, cost control, and patient-centered care while addressing the challenges of healthcare data integration and risk management. Healthcare providers are assessed based on quality measures, such as patient outcomes, safety, patient experience, and care coordination. For example, compensation is reduced if a patient has to be readmitted to the emergency room for the same reason. This idea of outcome-based pricing is not new, but is becoming more common. The idea was, in fact, pioneered by Rolls Royce in its "Power By The Hour" (PBTH) model. Rolls Royce only charged aircraft users when the engines were used, i.e., the aircraft was in the air. The buyers were not required to pay if the engine for in for maintenance or repair. This type of model can set the right incentives for both parties seeking common outcomes.

Subscription model for healthcare

Concierge medicine is a healthcare model that offers a personalized and premium level of medical care to patients in exchange for a fee or membership has become popular. In this model, patients typically pay an annual or monthly retainer to their chosen physician or medical practice. In return, they receive a range of benefits, including more extended and unhurried appointments, same-day or next-day access to their doctor, and often the ability to reach their physician via phone or email for medical advice. Concierge medicine allows doctors to limit the number of patients they see, leading to more focused attention on individual patient needs and comprehensive preventive care. In recent years, it has gained popularity among those seeking a higher level of personalized healthcare service. For example, the pricing is subscription-based and can vary based on age, if vaccinations are covered or not. Prices can vary from $100 to $10,000 a month.

As another example, in the book *Game Changer*,[12] BCG partner Jean-Manuel Izaret floats the idea of using a subscription model in healthcare insurance, claiming that it could improve access and health outcomes in a world where many curable diseases go untreated. A monthly subscription grants us access to a vast array of treatments. Healthcare could become far more affordable for many with a subscription payment plan. Rather than health insurance being solely responsible, the introduction of just a new pricing model could help significantly improve public health.

Taking Hepatitis C as an example, Izaret argues that this pricing model can address a major issue around the high cost of certain life-saving drugs. Although it is a curable infectious disease, many patients remain untreated due to the exorbitant cost of the drug on a per-patient basis. While the treatment saves money in the long term, it is often unaffordable in the short term. In the new model, instead of paying for individual treatments for each patient, health insurance providers or national healthcare systems would pay an annual fee to the companies for a specified number of years, granting them the right to treat all patients in need.

This model offers three significant benefits of creating a win–win solution. First, with a fixed fee arrangement for universal treatment, all patients would have immediate access to the required treatment. Second, by treating patients early – i.e., preventative care – the healthcare system will potentially reduce future treatment costs. Third, the model ensures a stable and predictable income stream for bio-pharmaceutical companies, allowing them to invest in research and development more confidently. The applications of this model can extend beyond infectious diseases. It can also work for expensive treatments that vary in severity across different patients, such as those for spinal muscular atrophy (SMA). By embracing a subscription model for medical treatments, we could revolutionize healthcare access and affordability, ultimately improving the quality of life for people worldwide.

Pricing for the Olympics

The London Olympics in 2012 dramatically changed the pricing model for ticket sales. Prior to this, tickets for the Olympics were expensive.[13] With an aim to strike a balance between generating revenue and ensuring broad access to the Games, it developed a new monetization schema. By increasing the range of ticket options and pricing structures, the organizers were able to accommodate a diverse audience while financially supporting the event's success. The HBR article "Pricing Lesson from the London Olympics" outlines some ideas that were implemented in 2012.

In previous Olympics, tickets for more popular sports like swimming were combined with those for less popular sports such as Tae kwon do. Historically, bundled ticket purchases often led to unused tickets for the secondary event. To address this issue, the committee opted to treat the ticketing of each sport independently, devising 26 distinct pricing plans that specified how tickets should be marketed and sold to their respective target audiences. Interestingly, though, the committee did incorporate public transportation costs into the ticket price, recognizing the opportunity to alleviate traffic congestion in and around the venues. This proactive pricing approach discouraged one behavior (non-attendance) while encouraging another (the use of public transportation), benefiting both spectators and the success of the Games. This is a good example of how bundled can be used strategically.

The organizers implemented tiered pricing, offering different price points for various events and seating categories. For example:

- Premium events like the opening and closing ceremonies, as well as popular sports like athletics and swimming, had higher ticket prices, while less popular events were more affordable.

- To encourage attendance and inclusivity, organizers made an effort to keep some tickets affordable, especially for events with high demand. This allowed a diverse audience, including families and individuals with different budgets, to attend the Games. Approximately 1.3 million tickets were made available as part of a "pay your age" promotion, catering to both young and elderly spectators. For those aged 16 or younger on the Games' commencement date, the ticket costs corresponded to their age in pounds. Conversely, individuals aged 60 or older on the same date enjoyed a fixed ticket price of £16.
- Early bird pricing was introduced to incentivize people to purchase tickets well in advance with lower prices. This idea was a novel one at that time.
- Dynamic pricing was used for some events. This means that ticket prices could fluctuate based on demand. When demand was high, prices could increase, and when demand was lower, prices could decrease. This helped balance attendance demand across different events.
- Special initiatives were introduced to ensure that local communities had access to affordable tickets. Programs like "Tickets for Schools" provided tickets to London schools, and "Tickets for Troops" offered free tickets to members of the armed forces.
- For those willing to pay more for a premium experience, special packages were available that included premium seating, hospitality, and other amenities. Organizers offered sponsorship packages and corporate hospitality options for businesses looking to entertain clients and associates during the Games.
- The pricing strategy also extended to the Paralympic Games, with a focus on making these events accessible and affordable for a wide audience.

Balancing revenue generation with the "purpose of inclusivity" enabled a diverse audience to enjoy the Olympic and Paralympic Games in London.

6. Cost engineering, aka target costing

Efficient supply chain investment

Pricing and supply chains are closely linked at many levels. During the pandemic, supply chains suffered significant disruptions, which led to empty shelves in stores and backlogs that lasted for two to three years. When a supply chain is disrupted, the cost of producing and transporting goods can increase significantly. This can raise prices for consumers as businesses pass on the additional costs. It's a classic case of demand and supply management.

Managing pricing in supply chain markets is critical. Another vital area of focus is innovation in the product and materials supply chains. This is where both prices can be impacted as well as its connection with societal good. Unilever, for example, has significantly reduced its raw materials cost by sourcing locally, reducing transportation costs. As we said in the introduction to this chapter, we aim to illustrate ways in which a company can reduce the costs of products that benefit society so that more people can afford them. Cost engineering is an integral part of this. The electric vehicle (EV) manufacturer Tesla is a pioneer of sustainable cost engineering. By developing its own battery technology and vertically integrating its supply chain, Tesla has reduced the cost of EV batteries while increasing their energy density.

Not just product innovation but managing production efficiently can also impact costs. Just-in-time (JIT) is a Japanese management philosophy that has been put into practice since the early 1970s in many Japanese manufacturing organizations. First developed and perfected within Toyota manufacturing plants by Taiichi Ohno, it became part of the Toyota Production System (TPS), where it is also known as Lean Manufacturing. Under JIT, instead of maintaining large inventories of parts and materials, Toyota parts and vehicles are produced only when needed. This reduces excess inventory, storage costs, and the waste associated with overproduction – all the while maintaining the goal of meeting consumer demands with minimum delays. Along with automation, JIT inventory management can reduce labor costs and increase efficiency – and therefore enable firms to offer lower prices to customers.

Transportation

On average, approximately 30% of product and service costs across the board can be attributed to a vehicle employed for delivery. As such, some optimization in this field could go a long way in reducing total costs while also reducing road traffic. Many consumer-packaged goods (CPG) companies, such as Georgia-Pacific, are exploring efficiencies with the goal of having fewer trucks on the road. One area for urgent attention is the last-mile delivery (the last part of a package's journey from a transportation hub to the customer's door), via retailers like Amazon, which is not an efficient stage as far as packaging and costs are concerned. Global logistics and courier company DHL, which is pursuing sustainability in its transportation operations, has a "GoGreen" program, under which it aims to reduce its greenhouse gas emissions by 50% by 2025 compared to 2007 levels. To achieve this, the company is investing in electric delivery vans and cargo bicycles for urban deliveries, thereby reducing emissions and congestion in urban areas. It is also exploring alternative fuels, optimization of delivery routes for efficiency, and green building practices for its facilities. IKEA is well known for its focus on sustainability and cost-conscious design in the furniture and home furnishings sector, which it revolutionized with its flat-pack packaging. This approach reduces shipping and storage costs and minimizes the carbon emissions associated with transportation and packaging.

A U.K. study compared the cost of shopping at a Walmart compared to Amazon and found that online purchases create more waste, as online items are more likely to come from different distribution centers. In fact, for some time, Walmart has been reducing its carbon footprint by optimizing transportation. The company launched a sustainability initiative as long ago as 2005, intending to reduce its greenhouse gas emissions by 20% by 2012. It optimized its transportation network by using more fuel-efficient vehicles, improved logistics planning, and implemented a training program to encourage more fuel-efficient driving. It also introduced a cross-docking system, where products are shipped directly from suppliers to stores without going through a distribution center, helping to reduce transportation distances and, therefore, emissions. These efforts helped Walmart to achieve its goal ahead of schedule, and the company has continued to make progress since. By 2019, it had reduced its greenhouse gas emissions by over 29% relative to its 2005 baseline, which was achieved through a combination of measures, including further transportation improvements, energy efficiency, and the use of renewable energy.

When supply chains reduce costs and become more efficient, quality improves, and prices can be significantly impacted. Innovations can mean reduced production and inventory costs for businesses, allowing them to offer lower prices to customers while remaining profitable. It is also worth bearing in mind that the cost reductions achieved through supply chain efficiencies have provided an opportunity for many companies to improve the environmental profile of their products.

Better partners

Sometimes the acquisition of better suppliers and partners, or better outcomes from negotiation, can drive a business model. In the GrassrootsLab case (see box), we discuss a purpose-led company that negotiated lower costs through its business delivery model, resulting in more affordable healthcare solutions.

Case: Lab tests anywhere, anytime

GrassrootsLab is an Atlanta-based company that seeks to align purpose, profit, and price. It's a digital health startup operating an online platform that allows individual consumers across the U.S. access to affordable blood testing services needed for outpatient medical care. Its target market is 56% of all Americans: in other words, 186 million underinsured people. In this context, "underinsured" means they either do not have health insurance or are on a high deductible/catastrophic health plan and are effectively cash-flowing all healthcare bills. GrassrootsLab's partners include health-sharing organizations and discount plan organizations, whose members benefit from the company's service. These organizations manage millions of members across the U.S., which includes those in the GrassrootsLab target market, and represent a total addressable market of approximately $1.825 billion.

GrassrootsLab increases access to healthcare by making it more straightforward, transparent, and reasonably priced – often 60–70% lower than comparable prices in the market; plus, its platform is user-friendly and easily accessible. The initial idea was that lab fees shouldn't be so high that they discourage people with chronic issues from purchasing regular blood tests. Lower prices results in more customers getting more tests done. In a study commissioned by the firm, one of their patients said,

> If I wanted to do tests that the doctor did not order, but I want to check my cholesterol or something like that, I can easily go on there and pay for it out of pocket and be more informed about what is going on with our bodies and then potentially save some money doing that.

Another said,

> …you take time off work for the first visit, then the bloodwork visit, and then the third is to go back to the doctor, to look at the bloodwork. That has always been frustrating…inefficient… goodbye to your money. [With GrassrootsLab] I can order the test and get the results back in 24 hours and be *aware* of what the results were.

The downstream impact of regular checking of chronic illnesses such as diabetes can be significant: fewer emergency care visits, fewer hospitalizations, and generally a higher quality of life at a lower cost for the patients themselves, for the insurance companies, and for society overall. Most importantly, GrassrootsLab's purpose and price are aligned and they have enabled this by better negotiation with the partners. High prices have always been a barrier for the majority of people. By removing them, GrassrootsLab encourages its members to take better care of their health and simplifies the process of getting the necessary blood tests needed for themselves and their families.

7. Green premium

As discussed in Chapter 3 on Innovation, the "green premium" is a strategy employed by many firms. Launching a product with a new stock-keeping unit (SKU) at a higher price has proved effective: for example, Clorox's Burt's Bees products, which retail at higher prices. But, as we have discussed elsewhere, higher prices limit wider adoption, and surely eco-friendly products should be more widely used? We explore this dilemma in detail below by revisiting Georgia-Pacific and looking at the case of its Brawny® paper towels.

Georgia-Pacific is one of the largest paper towel manufacturers in the U.S. It produces some of North America's most prominent consumer paper product lines, including Brawny®, Sparkle®, Quilted Northern®, Angel Soft®, and Dixie®. Brawny is its premium paper towel product, but it has recently seen increased competition and pricing pressure from private-label branded products, causing its market share to shrink. Meanwhile, eco-awareness has become a prominent selling point for household product shoppers. Georgia-Pacific believed that, by replacing its existing Brawny® line with a 100% compostable product, it could increase the number of households using its product and differentiate itself in a crowded market.

However, there was concern about alienating the existing Brawny® consumer base. The company needed to understand consumers' willingness to pay for this type of product, their perceptions of and hesitancies around sustainable household products, and how to effectively communicate the change should it choose to go down this route.

Case: Georgia-Pacific: green premium – the price of sustainability

As the concern over environmental issues has grown, the U.S. Environmental Protection Agency (EPA) has imposed an increasing number of environmental regulations on large manufacturers such as Georgia-Pacific. This has coincided with the company's publicly declared positioning on sustainability as a company priority moving forward. It releases an annual Sustainability Report highlighting current projects, future goals, and recent awards and recognitions. Other initiatives related to this commitment are the development of sustainable packaging for its GP Pro materials, contributions to the conservation of wildlife and forestry, and efforts to reduce non-renewable resource use.

Most paper towel and ancillary tissue product use happens in the U.S.: approximately 7.8 million tons annually. It equates to roughly $8 billion in annual sales, and it is a top ten non-food category by dollars, buyers, and trips. U.S. household penetration is 87%. Let's look at this ubiquitous product through an environmentally conscious lens. Unsurprisingly, the process of manufacturing a paper towel starts with paper. Beginning with either virgin or recycled paper pulp extracted from wood or fiber, the pulp is cleaned, bleached, processed, dried, and scraped to the desired thickness. The remaining paper is then creped or embossed and rolled to size, where it can then be packaged and distributed. It is easy to see how quickly an entire nation could go through nearly 8 million tons of this product per year and, therefore, how harmful its unchecked manufacturing could be to the environment.

However, there are still some consumers who are skeptical of environmentally friendly products, and this is primarily for two reasons: (1) performance perception and (2) premium pricing. Both issues contribute significantly to delayed adoption. On average, an environmentally friendly product costs 25–39% more than a conventional one. Additionally, many consumers are doubtful whether a more sustainable product will yield the same quality as its non-sustainable counterpart. Companies try to address this through tactical communication, such as on in-store packaging or in advertising, with products often presented side by side to compare. However, performance skeptics remain and must be accounted for when companies consider introducing new products or changing existing product lines to eco-friendly products.

Competition

The consumer market for paper towels is highly fragmented, with a range of players such as Procter & Gamble (P&G), Georgia-Pacific, Kimberly-Clark, SCA, Cascades, Kruger, Metsä Tissue, Hengan, WEPA, Asaleo Care, C&S Paper, Essendant Inc (Boardwalk), Oasis Brands, Seventh Generation, and private-label brands. Among these, P&G is the leading global supplier, and the market can be divided across performance tiers: premium, mainstream, and economy.

The economy tier, which includes brands such as FIORA®, Seventh Generation, and Marcal, is the one with the lowest price point. These brands generally offer lower performance across absorbency, strength, and softness. This tier typically accounts for 16–17% of paper towel dollar share. The mainstream level, including brands such as Sparkle®, Bounty® Essentials, and Scott®, is generally priced higher and performs slightly better than the economy products. It accounts for 30–32% of the paper towel dollar share. The premium level, which includes brands such as Bounty®, Brawny®, and Viva®, is priced the highest, offering the best performance, largest roll size, and variety of sheet types. This tier is primarily dominated by P&G's Bounty®, which holds roughly a 40% market share.

Within each of these tiers, e-commerce brands (e.g., Amazon), club stores (e.g., Costco, Sam's Club), mass-market stores (e.g., Walmart, Target), grocery stores (e.g., Kroger, Publix), drug stores (e.g., CVS, Walgreens), and dollar stores (e.g., Dollar General) have competing private-label products. These private-label competitors have seen tremendous growth in recent years; as pricing is often more competitive, differentiation between products is minimal, and consumer engagement is low.

Analysis

Here is a breakdown of the main concerns facing Georgia-Pacific with regard to the market:

- Private-label threat. As with many other household products, retailers have begun to realize the price sensitivity of consumers in this space, along with the low overall consumer engagement. This has culminated in a private-label threat, as retailers can control shelf space to drive down comparable product prices while keeping margins attractive. This trend has continued, growing rapidly in recent years.
- Brawny® product positioning. Within the three distinct tiers of the paper towel market Brawny® is positioned as premium, emphasis being placed on its strength and its unique "tear-a-square" feature, while being priced competitively with peer brands such as Viva and Bounty.
- Environmental issues and focus. Environmental activism has had a big impact on consumer purchasing habits. For large manufacturers, this has meant adapting to changes in government regulations and tailoring products and perceptions. As discussed, Georgia-Pacific has placed a priority on this.
- Appeasing customers and consumers. The dynamic of the retail value chain is such that paper manufacturers, such as Georgia-Pacific, must prioritize the needs of both their direct customers (retailers) as well as their end-consumers. But manufacturers don't have control over final pricing for consumers and can only set an MSRP (manufacturer's suggested retail price). However, there are advantages to this dynamic. In some circumstances,

retailers can work alongside manufacturers to help set corporate goals, such as purpose-related initiatives. Manufacturers thereby gain additional leverage and can find creative ways to ensure a consistent customer relationship.

• Consumer segmentation. An option here is to take a value-based approach using sustainability as a value driven. By creating unique consumer segmentations through statistical analysis these can then be used to target the desired consumers more effectively through communication strategies and position the new product alongside competitive options. A survey of over 1,000 respondents assessed willingness to pay, performance perceptions, and messaging tactics.

Findings

Based on the segmentation analysis, customers can be broadly grouped into four segments based on willingness to pay for perceived environmentally friendly products (see Figure 9.1).

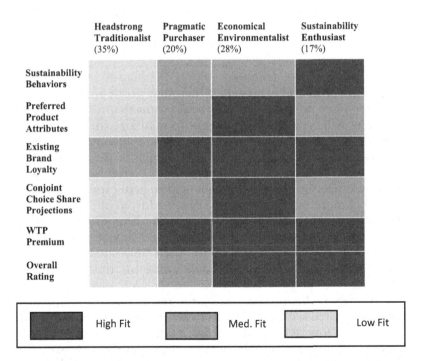

Figure 9.1 Segments based on survey data analysis. Segment fit for Brawny based on conjoint analysis.

I. Sustainability Enthusiasts (17% market): Customers will pay 15% more for the product.
II. Economical Environmentalist (28% market): Customers who would not pay more but at the same price buy the compostable product.
III. Pragmatic Purchaser (20% market): Customers that would buy the cheapest product or customers that would buy the eco product if the price was lower than the conventional product.
IV. Headstrong (35% market): Customers that will not change brands; Customers that think eco-products are low-performing and have minimal impact on the environment; Customers that believe global warming is a hoax.

The dilemma

The results from the survey pointed toward two alternatives that were similar from a financial standpoint:

1. Price the product 3% higher. Replace the current SKU with a compostable line.
2. A potential gain in share of 1.5% but no change in price. Replace the current SKU with a compostable line but at the same price.

Discussion

Most companies today introduce their new green product lines at a higher price to maximize the new product's profit margin. A company will typically also attempt to minimize the cannibalization of the conventional product. Suppose the company reduces the price of the purpose product to be similar to the conventional product. In that case, it can fully replace its conventional line with the environmental version, which would be better for the planet as it reaches more buyers. As can be observed from our calculations, the difference between the impacts on the bottom line between Alternative 1 (more buyers) and Alternative 2 (higher price) is minimal. Alternative 1 is, therefore, the preferable choice: better for the environment, with more people going for the compostable product.

However, if this product had large research and development costs associated with it, or it was expensive to make based on the cost and/or low availability of raw materials, we recommend a slightly different strategy. In such a case, we expect companies to price at a premium to establish the product market fit and market the product to customers in the "Sustainability Enthusiasts" segment who are willing to pay a higher price. The composability benefit is a value driver for these people, who are 17% of the population. If you recollect from Chapter 3, this would be innovators and early adopters in the innovation diffusion model. Once this segment is established, R&D costs are recouped, and prices can be reduced; the segment to go after would be the "Economical Environmentalist," which comprises 28% of the population. They value sustainability but are unwilling to pay a large price premium for the product. Once this segment is secured, the next segment to target is the "Pragmatic Purchaser." This segment comprises 20% of the market and enjoys the thought of acting sustainably but prioritizes traditional products to stay under budget. The price for this segment needs to be at par with the conventional product price, and the firm will need to work hard to convince this buyer that there are no performance issues with the new eco-line. The last segment, the "Headstrong Traditionalist," is 35% of the market and may only start buying the product once it is mainstream and maybe even the only product available. At this time, the company will be best served to remove the conventional line and price the compostable product on or below the conventional product to push the switch. Refer to Chapter 3 to further understand how to manage products in the last lifecycle stage.

In this section, we provide a summary of pricing strategies that can assist in maintaining a firm's financial viability while aligning with its purpose. Some strategies, like cost engineering, are oriented toward the long term, while others, such as bundling and unbundling, constitute short-term objectives for managers and serve as an interim solution for firms to survive and transform fully into purpose-driven organizations.

Last words

Pricing and purpose can be closely linked. Companies that effectively balance both value capture and creation can gain a significant competitive advantage by experimenting, remaining flexible, focusing on customer value, and leveraging price. In summary, pricing is a critical component of actualizing purpose and is vital in determining the commercial success of new products, services, or business models. Remember that doing good for society and the planet is at the heart of a purpose-driven firm. Companies that can effectively create customer and societal value will be able to thrive and compete in the future. Pricing will be critical lever to accelerate towards this goal.

Notes

1 Raj Sisodia, Jag Sheth, and David B. Wolfe, *Firms of Endearment: How World-Class Companies Profit from Passion and Purpose* (1st edn; Wharton School Publishing/Pearson Education, 2007).

2 Jonathan Chadwick, "Apple's 2020 iPhones May Come without a Power Adapter or EarPods in the Box as the U.S. Tech Giant Looks to Offset the Cost of Adding 5G Support to Its Next-Generation Handsets." DailyMail.com, June 29, 2020. https://www.dailymail.co.uk/sciencetech/article-8470069/Leaker-says-new-iPhones-wont-include-EarPods-power-adaptor.html

3 "Here Is How Apple Made an Extra $6.5 Billion by One Simple Decision." The Useful Tech, March 18, 2022. https://medium.com/the-useful-tech/here-is-how-apple-made-an-extra-6-5-billion-by-one-simple-decision-ab8fa03fb5d3

4 Deloitte Consulting LLP, *Unbundle Products and Services: Giving You Just What You Want, Nothing More.* 2015. https://www2.deloitte.com/content/dam/insights/us/articles/disruptive-strategy-unbundling-strategy-standalone-products/DUP_3033_Unbundle-products_v2.pdf

5 "Unbundling Harvard: How the Traditional University Is Being Disrupted." CB Insights, November 5, 2020. https://www.cbinsights.com/research/edtech-companies-unbundling-university

6 "Endlessly Refreshing: Coca-Cola North America Rolls out Bottles Made from 100% Recycled PET Plastic." The Coca Cola Company, February 10, 2021. https://www.coca-colacompany.com/media-center/packaging-sustainability-in-united-states

7 C.K. Prahalad, *The Fortune at the Bottom of the Pyramid: Eradicating Poverty through Profits* (1st edn; Wharton School Publishing, 2004).

8 B. Chakravarthy and S. Coughlan, "Emerging Market Strategy: Innovating both Products and Delivery Systems." *Strategy & Leadership* 40(1) (2012): 27–32.

9 P. Moscibrodzki, M. Dobelle, J. Stone, C. Kalumuna, Y.-H.M. Chiu, and N. Hennig, "Free versus Purchased Mosquito Net Ownership and Use in Budondo Sub-county, Uganda." *Malaria Journal* 17(363) (2018). https://doi.org/10.1186/s12936-018-2515-y

10 Donald Shoup, "The High Cost of Free Parking with Donald Shoup." *The War on Cars Podcast*, January 17, 2023. https://thewaroncars.org/2023/01/17/the-high-cost-of-free-parking-with-donald-shoup

11 Donald Shoup, *The High Cost of Free Parking* (rev. updated edn; Routledge, 2011).

12 Jean-Manuel Izaret and Arnab Sinha, *Game Changer: How Strategic Pricing Shapes Businesses, Markets, and Society* (1st ed. Wiley, 2023).

13 Marco Bertini and John T. Gourville, "Pricing Lessons from the London Olympics." *Harvard Business Review*, June 19, 2012.

Index

Pages in *italics* refer to figures and pages in **bold** refer to tables.

goals 118; inflation and 120; reducing plastic waste 8; renewable energy 8; RFID tagging 106; supply chain 8; sustainable sourcing practices 8; targets for recycled packaging content 106
warranties 64
water tariffs 84
Weber, Ernst 57
Weber–Fechner experiments 57
Wendy's 95
Westerveld, Jay 96
WestRock 117

Whole Foods Market 120
Williams, Freya 44, 47
woke capitalism 3
World Health Organization (WHO) 81
World Trade Organization 71
"Worn Wear" program (Patagonia) 125

Yoplait 95

zero-emission vehicles (ZEV) 74; *see also* electric vehicle (EV)

Printed in the United States
by Baker & Taylor Publisher Services